The Conglomerate Commotion

The Conglomerate Commotion

By the Editors of FORTUNE

NEW YORK / THE VIKING PRESS

First published in 1970 in a hardbound edition
and a Viking Compass edition by
The Viking Press, Inc.,
625 Madison Avenue, New York, N.Y. 10022

Published simultaneously in Canada by
The Macmillan Company of Canada Limited

SBN 670–23716–7 hardbound
670–00296–8 Viking Compass edition

Library of Congress catalog card number: 79–104152

Printed in U.S.A.

CONTENTS

Introduction

LOOKING BACK ON the 1960s, an observer of the business scene in the United States would almost certainly conclude that the most important continuing business story of the decade was the explosive irruption of the conglomerates— multi-market companies that grow, to a great extent, by acquiring other companies. *Fortune* covered that lively and sometimes adventuresome story as it unfolded, reporting the successes and stumbles of individual conglomerates and occasionally taking a broad look at the conglomerate commotion. A selected dozen or so of those reports and broader examinations make up this book. Except for the first two, the chapters are basically independent of each other, and readers so inclined may browse among them at will. But while the book is an anthology, it is a structured anthology, with the chapters arranged in a considered order.

The book is divided into three parts. The first two chapters of Part I provide an over-all view of the conglomerates as a group. Then come four accounts of multi-product companies in more or less happy, or at least hopeful, circumstances: Textron, Litton Industries, Gulf & Western, and W. R. Grace.

While the mood of Part I is distinctly positive, that of Part II is on the somber side. Two chapters, written two years apart by the same *Fortune* staffer (Gilbert Burck), are somewhat skeptical examinations of the conglomerate phenomenon. The other two chapters are accounts of conglomerates that ran into unhappy days: Litton Industries, on its bump down to death, and the corporation formerly known as "Automatic" Sprinkler (now A-T-O Inc.).

Part III, "Offense and Defense," begins with a compact manual of the strategy and tactics of fending off a take-over. It is followed by two case histories of eventful corporate struggles, one in which an acquirer finally took over the target company and one in which the target company succeeded in beating back the would-be acquirer.

Some of the original articles have been slightly abridged, but otherwise the chapters appear here pretty much as they first appeared in print, without benefit of hindsight. At the beginning of each chapter appears the date of publication in *Fortune,* and readers are urged to take note of it; some chapters contain time references such as "last year" and "recently" that relate to the original date. A majority of the chapters were originally published in 1968 or 1969, but some appeared earlier, and one goes back to 1964. Since we have not made substantive alterations in the original texts, some of the less recent chapters are no longer meant to be read as current reports. The subject of the least recent, Textron, has changed quite a lot since 1964—it has shucked off some divisions and products and added others, installed a new chief executive (G. William Miller), and more than doubled in total sales. Yet the Textron chapter, beyond its value as history, is still instructive, and the central point— that it takes good managing to manage a conglomerate—has held up well. In subsequent chapters readers will find that point recurring.

The efforts of a large number of people went into this book, but four in particular made major contributions: Stanley H. Brown, Gilbert Burck, Thomas O'Hanlon, and William Simon Rukeyser, each of whom wrote at least two of the chapters. Other parts were written by John Davenport, Daniel Seligman, and T. A. Wise. Assisting as research associates were Lucie Adam, Eleanore Carruth, Lorraine Carson, Ann Hengstenberg, Patricia Hough, Marjorie Jack, Wyndham Robertson, Edith Roper, and Ann Scott. The charts in their original form in *Fortune* were the work of Alexander Semenoick. Helen Donovan and Judy Grape helped prepare the pages for publication in book form.

The Editors of *Fortune*

PART I

Corporations
in Motion

This brief first chapter is a somewhat abridged version of an editorial from the June 15, 1967, issue of *Fortune,* which contained that year's directory of the 500 largest U.S. industrial corporations. The following chapter, from the same issue, should be read as a companion piece. Despite its location at the beginning of the book, this first chapter should not be thought of as a tone-setting preface to all subsequent chapters—as readers will see, there is a variety of tones.

The Case for Conglomerates

THE WORD "conglomerate" lands on the business pages with monotonous regularity these days; indeed, a case might be made that conglomerates are the most important current trend in the universe of big business. What is involved is the increasing tendency of large corporations to diversify, not just horizontally (into related products), or vertically (into products of suppliers or customers), but into many different products that may be quite unrelated to those previously produced. A preponderance of the talk about this trend seems to be about the problems associated with it, rather than the opportunities, and plainly reflects a deep-seated hostility to conglomerates. The term itself is rather tendentious, implying some special lack of form and logic, and its pejorative connotations may be one reason that the businessmen most prominently identified as heads of conglomerates spend so much time arguing defensively that they really aren't.

However, there are some other pretty good reasons for being defensive: anyone embracing the term in public will find that he has critics and regulators swarming all over him. From within the Justice Department come persistent vibrations suggesting that conglomeration presents an antitrust problem—although the exact nature of the problem remains rather murky. Conglomerates are frequently assailed as stock

3

promotions, and from the financial community, not to mention the Securities and Exchange Commission, have come recurring demands that they be required to report in more detail than other companies. Among academics and management consultants, there is a widespread view that conglomerates present unique management problems, and that many of them will end up in big trouble. Related to several of these views is a stubborn conservative prejudice to the effect that conglomerates are just "unnatural," that there is some kind of inherent impropriety in companies taking on unrelated ventures, that if God had wanted I.T.T. to be in the automobile rental business He would have made it that way.

Much of the discussion about conglomerates rests on misapprehensions. Despite all the news about unrelated diversification, conglomerates are far less prevalent than one might think. Taken as a group, furthermore, they are neither as powerful as some trustbusters seem to think they are nor as problem-ridden as some of their other critics believe. By what is ultimately the best measure of corporate success, long-term growth in earnings per share, conglomerates as a group do about as well as other companies. However, it does appear that certain kinds of conglomerates—those that have made diversification a "way of life," rather than just a response to trouble—are able to generate superior earnings performance fairly consistently.

Some of the arguments being pushed at conglomerates nowadays suggest that the pushers just don't like them—no matter what the data show. Why, for example, are conglomerates viewed as a threat to competition? It is clear that opinion makers inside the Justice Department are not agreed on the answer to that question, and perhaps that is why outsiders have so much trouble getting a straight answer. Donald F. Turner, the head of the Antitrust Division, has several times been quoted to the effect that conglomerate mergers are a problem, but not a major problem. Well, then, what is the *minor* problem? Justice Department spokesmen have offered several possible scenarios involving problems; most of them seem to be derived from Turner's own massive study of the subject, published in the *Harvard Law Review* at just about the time he was named head of the division. There is a problem, for example, involving reciprocity: one division of a conglomerate might have a competitive advantage in selling a customer who was, in turn, an important supplier to another division. Another scenario has a large and powerful conglomerate moving into a market previously divided among many small competitors, and using its financial resources to drive the others out of business. Alternatively, a conglomerate might gain competitive advantage from its ability to accept losses in one market, making them up with profits in others.

All these scenarios have a surface plausibility. But all of them involve what in formal logic is called the "fallacy of accident": the antitrust offense is clear enough, but the fact that the offender is a conglomerate is accidental and irrelevant; the real problem in each case is a pattern of behavior that conglomerates might or might not follow—as might companies in only one or two industries.

The fallacy of accident also turns up in several other kinds of criticisms that are recurrently thrown at conglomerates. The notion that they are apt to be stock promotions may have its roots in the operations of some flamboyant "raiders" of the 1950s, who worked hard at finding undervalued situations and seemed willing to buy situations in just about any industry. In any case, the unhappy experiences of a fair number of companies—they include Bellanca, Penn-Texas, and Merritt-Chapman & Scott—got the investing public to make a mental association between wide diversification and heavy touting of a weak company's stock. The association was doubtless reinforced by the case of Westec Corp., which was in oil and gas exploration, real estate, aerospace equipment, and geophysical instruments at the time of its scandalous bankruptcy. The mental association is natural and understandable. But the fact is that other heavily diversified companies, built on a long series of acquisitions, have done just beautifully, sustaining powerful earnings records over long periods of time; Litton, Textron, I.T.T., and Indian Head are examples that come to mind. What is critical, of course, is management, and there is no good reason to identify diversification with poor management, or with a management that overworks the promotion of its stock.

Should multi-market companies be required to report in more detail than they now do? Maybe they should—but the reasons advanced apply to a great many companies that aren't ordinarily thought of as conglomerates, and their advancement suggests, again, the extent of prejudice against conglomerates. The main contention, of course, is that when a company is in many different markets and industries, it is hard for investors to have any clear idea where the profits are coming from. If the object is to let investors in on what's making money, and what isn't, and what the amounts are, then the discussion covers just about all multi-divisional companies; in fact, the requirement would seem to call for some reporting *within* particular divisions. The Edsel, it may be remembered, was just part of the M-E-L Division while it was losing several hundred million dollars for the Ford Motor Co. A drug company with hundreds of products may have its profits heavily concentrated in just one of them.

Of all the questions insistently raised about conglomerates, the oddest in a way is the one about their "workability." The oddity resides in the proved fact that many conglomerates do work, and that some of them, as we have observed, have long records of consistent earnings gains. It is certainly fair to argue that there are special problems involved in managing conglomerates. But many have gone from the problems to an assertion, or at least implication, that there will come a day of reckoning, in which the management problems of many conglomerates will finally catch up with them. The most plausible part of the case is the thought that, at some point in the diversification process, top management finds it is in so many businesses that it cannot possibly have a "feel" for all of them. "The greatest danger in diversification," said Stanley S. Miller in his influential volume, *The Management Problems of Diversification,* "is that it tends to separate management talents and interests from the everyday content of a particular business environment."

The danger is real; the fact remains that most large diversified corporations have been able to surmount it. Chairman Birny Mason Jr. of Union Carbide, which is heavily diversified, explained how his company had worked to minimize the danger, and added: "I confidently feel, if you give me a decent period of time, I can tell you almost anything that is going on around the world in Union Carbide Corporation. Not only can I do it, but at least twelve of our top people can."

At this point it will pay to inquire why, if conglomerates are so unpopular in so many different quarters, the trend to conglomeration is nevertheless so powerful. The answer must be that the diversifiers in question are more concerned with their profits than with their popularity. But haven't businessmen *always* been concerned with their profits? In a sense, the answer is no, they haven't always; at least, the concern in recent years has been far more sharply focused and systematic than it used to be. Heavily influenced by the advent of computers, and the related requirement to engage in organized long-term planning, businessmen have increasingly found themselves in an environment dominated by the "systems" approach to decision making. The approach forces decision makers to keep on asking themselves about their ultimate objectives and to keep on challenging any conventional notions about the way to achieve them.

The effect of these new modes of thought has clearly been devastating in many industries. Formerly, men in, say, the cement business knew exactly what to do with their profits: pay out part of them to stockholders and reinvest most of the balance in cement plants. But anyone who sets out to clarify his ultimate objective comes, fairly rapidly, to the proposition that his main objective is maximizing the return on his capital and, thereby, raising the value of his stock. And when he gets to *that*, he proceeds inexorably to the thought that alternate investments may yield higher payoffs than cement. When he gets used to the idea that alternate investments are not only legal and moral, but profitable, he is pretty far along the road to becoming a conglomerator.

In short, the critics of conglomeration who view it as an irrational and aberrant development in business history, or as just the latest fad on Wall Street, are missing the point. The diversifiers are far more rational than those businessmen who are, so to speak, stuck in cement.

The Odd News about Conglomerates

THE SO-CALLED "conglomerate" has been one of the more controversial sights on the business landscape in recent years. The term usually refers to corporations operating in a number of different, unrelated markets; and there is no doubt that the number of such corporations has been rising quite sharply. About 60 percent of the 1,517 mergers reported by the Federal Trade Commission last year were across broad industry lines. The controversies enveloping these new kinds of enterprises are numerous, but a lot of the controversy seems to be based on misapprehensions. For one thing, the prevalence of conglomerates has been greatly overstated. For another, it appears that there is actually very little difference in the earnings performance of conglomerates and other companies.

These are the main conclusions derived from a special *Fortune* analysis of the companies on this year's list of the 500 largest U.S. industrial corporations. Specifically, two questions were examined: First, how many major industries does each of the 500 operate in? Second, what is the relationship between the extent of diversification and the growth of earnings per share? To make the answers meaningful, it is necessary to consider the way in which the analysis was conducted.

The Bureau of the Budget publishes a volume called

8

Standard Industrial Classification Manual, which identifies seventy-eight major categories of business. Manufacturing accounts for twenty-one of the categories, many of which are quite broad ("machinery, except electrical," for example, refers to the manufacture of everything from tractors to computers). There are also five mining categories in the manual. The "industry medians" that summarize the performance of the 500 are derived from these S.I.C. categories, although over the years we have modified or combined some of them; mining, for example, is considered only one industry in calculating the medians. The other fifty-two categories listed in the manual involve a diverse assortment of businesses. For the purpose of this analysis, some of the categories seemed too broad to be useful and were broken up: miscellaneous business services, for example, was broken into computer services, engineering services, and "other." At the present time, it seemed reasonable to ignore many of the categories (e.g., nonprofit organizations) because none of the 500 were involved in them, and to consolidate others that seemed fairly similar (e.g., paper and wood products). In the end, we came out with twenty-eight nonindustrial categories and twenty-six industrial categories; it was these fifty-four that were matched against the operations of the 500.

The first, rather startling finding is that conglomeration is still very much the exception, not the rule. Diversification across broad industry lines is not nearly so common as might have been supposed from all those headlines about mergers and acquisitions in recent years. On *Fortune's* definitions, 102 of the 500 are still operating in a single category. Many of these companies have achieved some diversification within their categories, of course, particularly in such broad categories as food, textiles, and electrical machinery. Nonetheless, these 102 are mostly still committed to their traditional markets.

Furthermore, as the distribution chart on page 11 makes clear, most of the companies in more than one category are still not in very many; eighty-nine companies are in just two categories, seventy-four are in just three, and seventy-two are in just four. How many categories does it take to attain conglomerate status? Any answer is necessarily somewhat arbitrary and subjective; readers who may have firm notions about the right answer are invited to use the chart to determine for themselves how many of the 500 are conglomerates. Meanwhile, let us assume that *eight* categories implies conglomeration. On that assumption, there are forty-six conglomerates on the list. The most diversified of them all is Litton, which is in eighteen categories; General Tire & Rubber is in seventeen (but would be in twenty-five, and would therefore be the most conglomerated of all, if the operations of its non-consolidated subsidiaries were counted). It may come as a surprise that the company in fourteen categories is General Electric. And that both Armour and Brunswick are in eleven, and Ford in eight.

What about the relationship between diversification and growth in earnings per share? To get at this question, we did a correlation analysis in which companies were assigned two variables: one was the number of industry categories; the other was the company's average annual growth (compounded) in per-share earnings between 1956 and 1966. (No attempt was made to derive growth rates for companies that had losses in either 1956 or 1966, and so the correlation analysis actually covered only 465 of the 500 companies.) The answer to the question is surprisingly negative; the coefficient of correlation turns out to be 0.086, a figure that is not statistically significant. In short, there isn't any relationship to speak of between diversification and earnings growth. The median growth rate for companies in eight or more categories is 5.86 percent a year. By contrast, the median for the *least* diversified, or single-category companies, is 6.27 per-

---

How Many Do How Much?

The chart suggests that, despite the increasing numbers and scope of mergers in recent years, there is still a surprisingly low degree of diversification among the 500 largest industrials. The extent of diversification in each company was measured by assigning its business operations to one or more of fifty-four broad industry categories. The three most diversified companies—i.e., the three short bars at the right-hand side of the chart—are Litton Industries, General Tire & Rubber, and General Electric. But if a "conglomerate" is taken to be a company in at least eight categories, then only 9 percent of the companies can be considered conglomerates. More than 20 percent are in just one category.

Number of categories

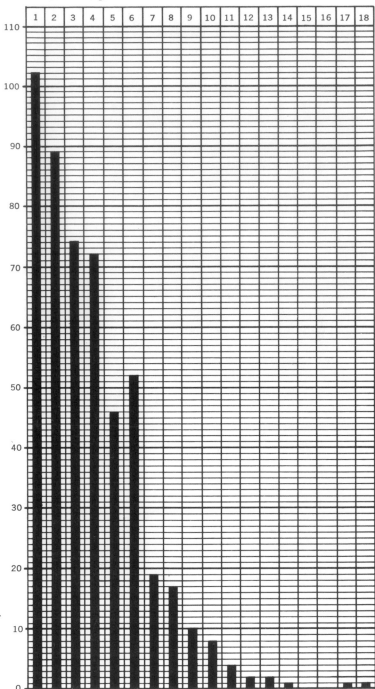

Number of companies

cent. The median for the 500 is 6.21 percent—but none of these deviations are statistically significant either.

The simple fact seems to be that there are a lot of different roads to growth. Litton's 36.53 percent annual average made it fourth among all the companies on the list; but none of the companies that beat it—in order, they were Westinghouse, Xerox, and Indian Head—are on the list of conglomerates.

Among other heavily diversified companies that turned in spectacular performances in earnings growth were Chrysler (nine categories), Fairchild Camera & Instrument (eight), I.B.M. (eight), and Texas Instruments (nine), all of whose compounded per-share earnings grew at better than 20 percent. But many of the conglomerates ranked poorly. Among these, Brunswick (eleven categories) had an earnings decline and Armour (eleven) actually showed a loss in 1966.

Of the single-category companies, meanwhile, eighteen had a ten-year average growth rate of better than 10 percent. Four of these, Avon, Collins & Aikman, Jonathan Logan, and Admiral, did better than 20 percent. Polaroid, the best performer of all among the single-category companies, ranks seventh among the 500 with an average rate of 28.34 percent.

Is the moral of the figures, then, that diversification is fruitless? The answer seems to be no, or at least not exactly; in any case, it will pay to look more closely at that list of conglomerates.

Two quite distinct patterns seem to be visible. Litton, Textron, FMC, and others have long been run on the assump-

---

Who Are the Conglomerates?

These forty-six companies are the most diversified in the United States —at least, they are if you accept the concepts and definitions on page 9. Taken together, their performance as to earnings growth in 1956–66 is not significantly different from that of others among the 500 largest industrials; but within this group there seems to be a discernible superiority for high-technology companies, and it persists when growth is measured only over the five years 1961–66. No growth rates are given if companies had a loss in either the first or last year of the period covered, or if per-share figures are unavailable (e.g., Farmland Industries, a cooperative). Figures in parentheses are negative.

Average annual growth in earnings per share

Company	Categories	1961-66	1956-66
Allied Chemical	9	7.54%	3.61%
American Cyanamid	9	12.92	4.90
Amer. Mach. & Foundry	10	(5.50)	5.35
Armour	11	—	—
Armstrong Cork	8	10.98	8.63
Avco	9	13.67	—
Bendix	10	8.02	3.17
Borden	9	8.35	5.86
Borg-Warner	12	14.28	2.28
Brunswick	11	(41.87)	(7.48)
Castle & Cooke	8	—	5.71
Chrysler	9	68.99	22.37
Consol. Electronics	8	14.35	2.08
Dow Chemical	10	13.72	6.15
Du Pont	9	(1.50)	.02
Eagle-Picher	8	21.98	1.79
Eltra	11	21.99	19.44
Evans Products	8	—	(3.72)
FMC	10	20.34	13.37
Fairchild Camera	8	15.47	24.54
Farmland Industries	8	—	—
Firestone Tire & Rubber	10	9.76	5.00
Ford Motor	8	8.76	9.96
General Dynamics	10	—	3.05
General Electric	14	6.58	4.28
General Precision	8	9.23	11.12
General Tire	17	12.43	15.15
Goodrich	8	9.31	.77
Goodyear	8	8.51	6.16
Grace (W.R.)	12	18.30	7.32
Gulf & Western	8	26.79	—
I.B.M.	8	19.22	20.63
I.T.T.	13	71.89	7.55
Johnson & Johnson	8	16.91	9.42
Kaiser Industries	8	28.56	1.18
Kidde (Walter)	11	—	4.03
Litton Industries	18	35.09	36.53
Lockheed Aircraft	10	15.76	11.80
Minnesota Mining & Mfg.	8	12.15	12.90
National Distillers	9	13.17	4.12
Ogden	9	29.36	1.59
Olin Mathieson	9	15.15	4.03
Rexall	10	13.45	12.43
Texas Instruments	9	27.09	26.90
Textron	13	27.93	16.15
Universal American	8	3.47	4.77

tion that just about all businesses, no matter how diverse, can be managed successfully by a small group of executives that coordinate accounting, planning, and financial services. Thus diversification is seen as a natural part of growth: it is not intended to afford protection against the loss of existing markets (although it may have that effect sometimes); it is not initiated because the company is in, or fears it may get in, trouble. It comes about quite naturally because the management views almost the whole business world as its oyster and feels essentially as free to take on new ventures as to invest in expanding old ones. At Litton, for example, half of sales growth in a typical year comes from acquisitions.

Meanwhile, a fair number of the other companies lodged among those conglomerates seem to have diversified defensively—i.e., because of present or potential problems with their business. This was certainly the case with Brunswick, whose troubles have been heavily centered in its original business, bowling equipment, and which has taken on a wide range of other enterprises—it is now in boats, school furniture, surgical instruments, and aircraft parts, among other things—but still has a poor ten-year record because of the miseries of the bowling business. Borden diversified, into chemicals, cosmetics, and fertilizers, because of its mounting concern over the low profit margins in the milk business; it too has a growth rate below the 500 median. Allied Chemical, with a weak 3.61 percent a year average, had a roughly parallel situation in its earlier dependence on bulk chemicals; it has been moving aggressively into textiles, plastics, and a number of other products. In several other companies too, it seems clear that the urge to diversify proceeded from a sense of concern about existing problems.

It is hard to quantify the case, but one hypothesis suggested by these examples is that the most successful of the conglomerates are relatively new companies that became conglomerates at some early stage in their development—rather than older companies that began diversifying heavily in response to problems and anxieties about the original corporate operations. Of the forty-six conglomerates listed on page 13, eighteen have average growth rates for the decade above 6.21 percent, which is the 500 median; two others,

Avco and Gulf & Western, went from a loss to a profit during the decade. On balance, the twenty seem to be somewhat "newer" companies, to have more roots in high technology, and to have fewer commitments to the past.

How to Manage
a Conglomerate

A TEXTRON EXECUTIVE named Jerome Ottmar left his house in Attleboro, Massachusetts, one day recently and set out on what was, for him, a routine business trip. He began by flying to a Textron plant in Gastonia, North Carolina, where he looked over some production equipment installed to manufacture a new chain saw. The next morning he drove with the Gastonia production manager across the state border to Greer, South Carolina, where the company has another plant. He talked with the manager there, and inspected facilities in which the company makes outboard motors and portable pumps and generators. Later that day he flew on to Augusta, Georgia, where Textron makes electric golf cars, for another fast conference. Toward the end of the day Ottmar flew down to Boca Raton, Florida, to visit a vacationing division president. Over the weekend they talked business, played golf, and then went to Boynton Beach, for a look at the company's marine-engine test station. On Monday morning Ottmar flew into New York for a meeting with the head of the company division that produces cold-flow metal parts and fasteners. They considered the possibility of a European venture and explored some licensing problems this would involve. Ottmar spent part of the next day at his desk in Providence, Rhode Island, where the company has its headquarters. Providence

16

is only a forty-minute drive from Attleboro, but Ottmar never did get home that night. Instead, he dined in Boston with some investment bankers who wanted a line on Textron's stock. The next day he flew to Montreal to help the management of one of Textron's Canadian companies with some plans to buy land and build a chain-saw, pump, and generator plant that would replace three others. That took the better part of two days, and Ottmar didn't get back home until Thursday night. The next day he was off again, this time to Springfield, Vermont, where Textron had just bought a major machine-tool maker. He met the president of the new unit and also the head of an older Textron division that makes machine tools. Together they began to discuss the delicate subject of eliminating duplicate products.

As all these problems and industries forcibly suggest, Ottmar works for a most unusual corporation. Actually, he is one of only three executive vice presidents; together they oversee twenty-seven separate divisions and 113 plants. Although Textron is still often thought of as the textile company founded by the famous entrepreneur, Royal Little, it is now completely out of textiles and in so many other lines that it cannot be identified by any one of them. Its most important single product is helicopters; the Bell Helicopter division, in Forth Worth, sold more than $100 million of them last year, principally the UH-1 for Army use in Vietnam. But helicopters represented less than 20 percent of sales, the rest being distributed over a large number of wildly dissimilar products.

Managing Textron is a unique business problem, but the job is done by only a handful of executives at headquarters in Providence. Headed by Rupert C. Thompson Jr., chairman and chief executive officer, Textron's supervisory and staff executives work in a small, simple suite of offices that look more like, say, the local branch office of a medium-sized insurance company than the executive offices of one of the largest United States industrials.

Thompson himself bristles at the word "conglomerate," with which, he says, his first and only association is "mess." (He suggests "non-related diversification.") His sensitivity seems to reflect a widespread feeling that Textron actually was something of a mess in years past. The present company was put together out of more than fifty different large and small corporate entities, and its direction has changed more than once.

Thompson's resistance to "conglomerate" also rests on a strong aversion to the frantic finance associated with some highly diversified companies.

The Conservative Conglomerators

Textron's own operations and finances have a distinctly unfrantic look about them. Although it sold its textile division a year ago (the unit had produced $71 million in sales in 1962), its total volume increased by 7 percent last year, from $549,493,000 in 1962 to $587,048,000; the current rate is about $650 million. Net income was up 22 percent to $18,047,000. The income figure was a company record, and especially significant because it was set in a year when Textron paid federal income taxes at the rate of about 44 percent, using up the last of its tax-loss credits. Thompson has suggested that 1964 earnings will set another record, probably reaching close to $20 million. Meanwhile, Textron's long-term debt is down to $33 million, obviously no great burden for a company with more than $150 million of stockholders' equity.

This conservative financial policy represents a considerable change at Textron. So, indeed, do Thompson's operating policies. All in all, his approach affords a stark contrast to the freewheeling ways of the promoter and builder who was his predecessor.

The company goes back to 1923, when Little founded an enterprise called Special Yarns Corp. It was strictly a textile company and remained one through twenty-nine years and three name changes. In 1944, Little renamed the company Textron, which he thought was modern-sounding and connoted both "textiles" and such synthetics as rayon and nylon. During World War II, Little set out to change the character of the company; in place of a simple textile manufacturer, he proposed to create a huge combine that would be completely integrated from raw fibers to finished apparel. By the end of 1949 he had his combine built—and discovered almost immediately that the concept would not work. The company was too big and slow-moving, and could not change the styles of its finished garments fast enough to compete with the hundreds of small dress manufacturers; unlike Textron, they were not tied to the long-term commitments and lead time of a company that wove and finished its own fabrics.

Undaunted, Little began to pull the company apart. In 1952 he got his stockholders to approve a charter change that would let him look outside the textile industry for future Textron acquisitions. He then took what looked like a step backward into textiles when he moved to take over American Woolen. The deal took more than a year to complete and *Fortune* called it "the stormiest merger yet." But American's huge tax-loss credits and bulging bag of liquid assets gave Little the money he needed to carry out his diversification program.

During the next five years Little bought most of the other units that now constitute Textron, making enough sound investments to cover his few big mistakes. His flamboyant methods continued to offend more conservative businessmen. Little himself recently recalled the time he tried to buy Brown & Bigelow, the calendar and advertising-specialty company, which, as it happened, was run by an ex-convict. "We got it approved by our board," Little said, "but when their board considered it, they didn't want to be associated with me."

As the conglomerated Textron began to assume its present shape, Little recognized that his real interest had been in putting it together. He didn't care for operations, and so he decided to bring in some people who did. Early in 1956 he persuaded a young Wall Street lawyer named George William Miller to leave Cravath, Swaine, & Moore and come to work for Textron. Miller is now Textron's president and chief operating officer. About the same time Little approached Thompson, who was an old friend, had been a Textron director for a time after the war, and had also been one of its bankers (at the Industrial National Bank in Providence). Thompson came on as vice chairman of the executive committee, taking over the management of Textron's nontextile divisions.

Little's acquisitions, for the most part, brought financially sound companies into Textron, most of them in manufacturing. He sought businesses with competent managements and insisted that these come along as part of any deal he made. One old associate recalls Little's emphasis on good management vividly. At one session he finally turned down a bargain-priced company with the observation, "If you had a decent management to run it, you wouldn't be giving it away."

Textron's new units generally could be supervised effectively by people who had only general experience in manufacturing. But acquisitions that required special backgrounds in other fields usually fared poorly. Textron got into one of these fields in 1956, when it bought the SS. *La Guardia*, a converted transport, from the federal government and chartered her to the Hawaiian Steamship Co., which renamed her the SS. *Leilani*. Little had intended the deal purely as an investment, and certainly had no interest in Textron's running the ship. But Hawaiian could not make her pay, and eventually defaulted on its payments. Textron did wind up running her, through a subsidiary of its own, Hawaiian Textron Inc. The company's 1957 annual report accordingly suggested that stockholders consider "a holiday to the Hawaiian Islands" and the *Leilani* "as an economical, carefree way to Hawaii." Not many stockholders took up the suggestion, however, and the federal government repossessed the ship after Textron had lost $2,300,000 operating her.

Textron's management learned that developing new inventions was not one of its strong points. The company tried to get into the photocopying business in 1960 by backing the inventor of a process called Photek. In 1961, Textron staked the operation to a brand-new plant. A year later Thompson decided to sell the division to a supplier after Textron had dropped $2 million on the venture. "Now you would have a hard time getting me to start from scratch with a company," said Thompson. "I'm a great believer in a record."

Textron has also had some large problems with an electronics subsidiary. Little had been shopping around for an electronics company for years, but had never found one whose stock did not seem overpriced (i.e., because of the high price-earnings ratios on electronics stocks). In May of 1959 he decided to solve this problem by *creating* one. Accordingly, Textron Electronics, Inc., was chartered. It immediately acquired from the parent company its MB

Manufacturing division, a former maker of mounts for propeller-driven aircraft engines that had switched to producing vibration-analysis and testing equipment. Subsequently, two other small Textron divisions were also sold to T.E.; Textron itself ended up owning 75 percent of the stock, with the rest publicly owned and traded on the American Stock Exchange. In 1959, the year it was formed, T.E.'s own price-earnings ratio went as high as 55 (vs. 9 for its parent), and this helped it to pick up a few other small outfits. However, the severe price cutting that plagued the industry in 1960–61, combined with internal management problems, created big losses and sent the stock tumbling.

A Bargain in Bell

When Little made his biggest acquisition—Bell Aircraft's defense business—word went around that he had finally been outfoxed. He had become concerned that Textron did not have enough government contracts. Defense was then about 8 percent of sales, most of it done through the Dalmo Victor division, which made airborne radar antennas. Little wanted to raise the figure to at least 20 percent. John E. Bierwirth, chairman of National Distillers and a former Textron director, brought Bell Aircraft to his attention (Bierwirth was also a Bell director). In July 1960, Textron concluded a deal for Bell's helicopter division, its rocket and guidance system maker, and a small manufacturer of servo controls.

The mistake was supposed to be the price Little had paid: $32 million for a business that in 1959 had earned only $4 million before taxes. However, Textron had put up only about half the purchase price in cash, the remainder having been borrowed by Bell Aerospace (as the business was renamed). In any case, the Bell earnings have risen sharply since Textron took over the properties. Thompson says, "We knew we had our objective—25 percent pretax on our investment—from day one." He admits, however, that he and Little had never expected anything like the huge increase in helicopter orders that added $50 million to Textron sales in 1963. All together, the Bell companies alone accounted for more than $160 million of corporate sales last year, more than a quarter of the total. Contract backlogs make it probable that these units will increase their sales and profits, despite the military cutback programs.

With Bell under Textron's belt, Little retired and Thompson took over as chief executive. At first he got Little to agree to hang around as chairman of the executive committee. But, Thompson says, Little never was much for committees and meetings. "The minute he wasn't going to run it alone, he left."

Thompson had started building his own operating system in 1958. "At first," he recalled recently, "I did it as Little did. Roy operated out of his hat." But that quickly proved unsatisfying for an ex-banker who liked things orderly and didn't like to be called at midnight by a division president with a problem. When Little left, Thompson quickly and quietly began making it clear that he was the boss and put the finishing touches on his own program of centralized control and divisional operation.

Its essentials were frankly copied from General Motors, whose management Thompson had studied carefully. Thompson also adapted the G.M. concept of relating the profits from any venture to the invested capital it required. Return on investment is the standard applied to each of Textron's diverse operations. It is a standard applied consistently and unsentimentally.

One unsentimental move was made about a year ago, when Thompson took the Textron company completely out of its original business. This happened when it sold its Amerotron textile division to Deering-Milliken for $45 million. Amerotron, an efficient textile operation, was returning only about 11 percent on investment (before taxes). "We felt we could make more by investing that textile money in other types of businesses," Thompson said recently. He used the proceeds of the sale to cut the company's long-term debt, to increase the working capital of some fast-growing divisions, and to pick up a few more companies, including Jones & Lamson, the Vermont machine-tool maker.

Thompson expects Textron's money to earn a lot more than 11 percent before taxes. Indeed, he insists that a 25 percent return (i.e., operating profit before taxes or corporate charges) be immediately attainable, or at least clearly foreseeable, in any company Textron buys. All Textron divisions taken together are averaging about that right now. On an after-tax basis the company has been doing better than big United States industrials in general, whose median return on invested capital has run under 9 percent in recent years. Little once set a long-term corporate objective of 20 percent after taxes for Textron, on the rather ambitious premise that Textron should do as well as General Motors in this respect. Thompson now regards that objective as "somewhat lofty."

To ensure that the divisions attain their investment objectives, Textron watches over their operations closely. "We foster the thought of autonomy," Thompson says, "but our association with the divisions is intimate." Thompson also says, frequently, "I don't like surprises." He wants the divisional forecasts to be realistic—and to be met. This is the responsibility of operating head Bill Miller. He has two principal means of minimizing surprises: one is the monthly, quarterly, and annual budgets, forecasts, and reports that each division must submit to Providence; the other is the fieldwork of the three executive vice presidents and the other group executives.

The divisional reports are detailed ones. Division presidents are responsible for submitting and sticking to annual budgets, complete to such details as contributions to a local community fund. They can hire personnel and fix salaries themselves only under the $15,000 level. Capital expenditures of more than $5,000 must be approved by Providence. If they involve assets of $25,000 or more, they get a careful second look six months after the facility has been installed; a post-completion report must then be made, detailing the operating economics of the item and the actual return on investment. Depending on their size, appropriations for personnel or capital must be approved by the division's group executive, by its executive vice president, by Thompson and Miller personally, or by the executive committee of Textron's board. (Since the executive committee meets twice a month, no division ever has to wait very long before getting what it needs.) Providence must also be notified of any *sale* of a fixed asset, and must approve those involving more than $5,000. Not very surprisingly, much of the humor at Textron's top executive level turns on the vigilance exercised by the boss in watching over the dollars. Thompson's executives kid him about his alleged slowness in reaching for dinner checks, and he repeatedly reminds them, half seriously, of the old New England motto, "Use it up; wear it out; make it do; or do without."

Divisional operating figures and forecasts are formally reviewed by headquarters management once a month. The scene of the review is a room on the second floor of Providence's Hope Club, on the corner of Benefit and Benevolent streets. Despite the number and variety of divisions, these meetings are generally finished in half a day, with most of Thompson's and Miller's attention given to the exceptional cases in which forecasts have not been met. "We manage by exception," Miller explained recently. He and Thompson do not rely only on the monthly meetings to keep abreast of divisional operations. They are in more frequent contact with any division that has something especially big in the works.

Checking Over the Homework

The other part of Miller's supervisory apparatus is the work of the three executive vice presidents, who report to him. Harvey Gaylord, who had been president of Bell Aircraft, oversees the defense group; the industrial and consumer products divisions are divided between Ottmar and Joseph Collinson. Ottmar and Collinson supervise some of their divisions personally, others through group executives, but both men spend about half their time on the road offering advice, putting out miscellaneous fires, keeping up with competitive developments, looking for new products, men, and ideas, and simply maintaining contact with division executives. "We expect the supervisors to know everyone in a division who is important, or will be," says Miller.

Ottmar was the first supervisor Thompson brought in. Trained as a chemical engineer, he had spent years as an executive of a New England concern called Metals & Controls and had been president of one of its divisions. On his own, Ottmar has interests in the profitable Attleboro *Sun* and in radio station WARA in Attleboro.

He sees his job with the divisions as "what a board of

directors would do, except that we're closer. I know the second level of management as well as the first, and I often know the third too. I go to the plants less often now because I know them well. If a new plant is to be constructed, I want to see the site and talk about the layout with the people planning it. That way I see how well they've done their homework."

Collinson's responsibilities are, if anything, more diverse than Ottmar's. He is a former banker and accountant, and served for more than three years as Textron's treasurer, a background he regards as ideal for his present assignment. "A finance man knows a little of everything," he remarked not long ago.

His big problems the past few years have been several new acquisitions; it has been his job to integrate them into the total Textron operation. A year ago, for example, Textron bought Continental Optical, primarily a lens maker and a logical partner for its Shuron division, a lens and frame manufacturer. Shuron itself had moved its lens manufacturing the previous year from upstate New York to a new plant in Barnwell, South Carolina. To bring Continental's operation into line with Shuron's, Collinson began, among other things, to arrange for closing one of the Continental plants, moving its equipment to another plant in Rochester, New York, and fusing the management groups from the two plants as painlessly as possible. Thus far, however, the profits of the Shuron Continental division are running below corporate management's expectations; Collinson's job is not finished.

Despite the tough reporting requirements, Textron's acquisitions have been delighted with the new association. In almost every case Textron had been able to buy them because their owners had some problem—often it involved a shortage of capital—that they couldn't solve themselves. When Textron bought Waterbury Farrel, for example, all but a small part of the production facilities were housed in a rambling collection of ancient buildings in downtown Waterbury, Connecticut. Textron quickly moved the operation to a new plant in nearby Cheshire (it was important to stay in the area so as to keep the skilled work force intact). More than a hundred old machine tools were replaced with fifty new ones. The company had needed the move and the new equipment years before, but had never been able to afford them.

A corporation as big and diverse as Textron, with so many unrelated divisions, probably could not be run successfully without a good incentive-compensation program, so that all the executives suddenly moved from a small to a big corporation can retain a belief in the importance of their own efforts. The divisional presidents select, although Providence must approve, the executives to be included in the program. They benefit to the extent that their divisions (or in some cases operations within a division) become "profit centers" and raise or hold Textron's return on its investment above a base level. Increases in compensation up to 100 percent of salary are possible under the program. One division man said recently, "Before Textron, we never thought about net worth, only about dollar income and return on sales." But the effect of the program—which may extend down to project engineers, shop managers, and purchasing agents—has been to permeate the entire corporation with an awareness of the return-on-investment concept. "It means our people request only the capital equipment which really pays for itself," says Carroll Martenson, head of the Hydraulic Research and Manufacturing Division.

One potential danger of emphasing return on investment is that managers may be tempted to raise one year's return at the expense of development programs that would pay off later. Corporate management is very much aware of the problem, but is satisfied that it hasn't been manifested yet. Thompson cites several new products and developments to prove that development programs have not been starved; they include Homelite's new XL-12 chain saw, for example, and the four-cycle outboard engine Homelite perfected after it had bounced around from one company to another for years. Thompson says the company will spend close to $9 million on product development this year, but he concedes that he doesn't intend to have Textron finance much basic research. Its most important forays into far-out research— e.g., Bell Aerosystems' developments in the fields of hovercraft and vertical-takeoff-and-landing planes (VTOL)—have been financed by government development contracts, which is the way Thompson likes it.

Aspiring to Blue-Chip Status

Textron is very much aware of Wall Street these days. Its management obviously feels it has a new and happy story to tell investors, and it is eager for investors to listen. The eagerness to publicize the company and its stock rests in part on an awareness that some acquisitions are in the works—Lon Casler, Textron's vice president for acquisitions, has a foot-high pile of prospect folders right now—and that any one of them would come cheaper if it could be paid for in a stock whose price-earnings ratio was higher. Thompson frankly aspires to blue-chip status for Textron, and the higher p/e's that would presumably come with it; and he has repeatedly suggested to the Street that it is underestimating Textron's potential.

Whether Textron ever does achieve blue-chip status will doubtless depend very largely on its ability to maintain earnings at a high level even in an economic downturn—a challenge the corporation in its present form has not yet faced. Since Textron is itself close to being a cross section of the industrial economy, any sharp downturn in industrial production would plainly pose a serious challenge to it. However, it has some special resources of its own to meet such challenges. One of them, of course, is the conservatism of its present finances. Its main resource, though, is that remarkably cool, efficient, and professional management in Providence.

This chapter is a somewhat condensed version of a 1966 dialogue between two members of the *Fortune* staff and two top executives of Litton Industries: Roy L. Ash, president, and Harry Gray, senior vice president (now executive vice president). As the introduction to the dialogue noted, Litton had been "one of the more spectacular business-success stories of recent years." Over the span from 1955 to 1965, the company's earnings per share had grown to an average rate of 44 percent a year, compounded. Another chapter on Litton, telling of its subsequent stumble, begins on page 109.

How Litton Keeps It Up

Litton's per-share earnings have been growing by over 30 percent a year for more than ten years now. The figure itself is phenomenal, but what's really mystified people about Litton, I think, is that it's had the growth without any of the usual trappings of a growth company. You don't have any big technological lock, like Xerox, and you're not one of those companies that are latched onto the population explosion, like Coca-Cola, say. How do you manage to keep it up?

ASH: Well, a part of the answer involves decisions we made years ago. One of our best decisions, which was also one of our very first, was not to enter the semiconductor business—this was back in late 1953. Relative to other objectives we had at that particular time, we felt it wasn't the time for us to enter that market.

What are some other things you looked at and decided against?

ASH: We were also considering certain atomic-energy applications and process-control computers during those years.

GRAY: The tough decision in atomic energy concerned radioisotopes—using the isotope thulium for x-rays. We had some very learned individuals in our company pressing us to get into the field, and we spent some money just to see what

29

was involved, what was the technology, and what was the market.

What was the total cost of making this analysis?
GRAY: The total dollar cost? I'd say $50,000.

ASH: I think the basic point is that we've always had a commercial perspective about our endeavors. Some companies have been much too technically oriented—technical accomplishment has been a goal in itself. Their *modus operandi* has been to work in the laboratory and come up with something technically exciting, and then try to sell it, before they've really had any idea at all whether there was a profit in it. But we always want to think in terms of the business potential.

In other words, you may decide not to bring something to market even after you've got the technology licked.

ASH: The timing is very important. Take the idea of applying microwave energy to heating and cooking. It was known twenty years ago that the concept could be made to work. We were working on the concept early ourselves, but we held off from marketing anything, even after others began; we wanted to be sure there was a commercial potential, not just an interesting, technically satisfying development. Today our Atherton Division leads that market.

Could you tell us in more detail—what had to happen before you decided it was time to go ahead there?

ASH: We looked at three different things. First, there was a critical decision to make about the technology itself. You often hear that the technical problems of this or that are licked, but sometimes that means they're licked only in the laboratory; there turn out to be major problems when you try to make the products work in the field. So that's the first test we applied. Then you have to examine the economics of the new product—all these kinds of products cross their technical feasibility threshold before they reach their economic feasibility threshold. And here again, when you talk about economics you've got to be clear it's not laboratory economics. In the laboratory people don't worry too much about the ultimate product cost and they're excited by novelty; in the marketplace the costs are crucial and the novelty wears off. Anyway, we finally got by that hurdle. The third question was one of public acceptance. The use of this new cooking technique was so different that it wasn't understood at first.

You mentioned that you weren't first in that market. General Sarnoff has made some digs about companies that let others pioneer, and then come in afterward—he was talking about color television, of course, but the implication was that the people who hadn't done the basic research, and then wanted to rush into the market, were sort of parasites. What's your response to that observation?

ASH: Well, we did as much basic research as anybody in this field; the point is that we just decided to enter it later, when the commercial problems had been solved. I believe in pioneering, but that doesn't have to mean being first. We all consider Columbus a pioneer even though others had set out before him—most of them were too early.

Does this type of situation occur often?

ASH: Many times in our history we've come to an early stage in a particular technological development and then said, "Let's assume we'll be able to complete the development of this product. Let's not spend the money yet, but just assume that we'll be totally successful." Assuming that, what would we do with the product? Is there a market? What is it? Can we reach it? How? Can the venture be profitable? Let's get those answers before we go back to perfecting the product.

It sounds as though this could be very discouraging to the man in the laboratory, who's been doing the experimental work—to be told to forget about finishing it because the analysis shows there's no market. What sort of drama took place when you called in the man who'd been working on the x-ray project and gave him the news?

GRAY: It was dramatic, I'd say.

What happened?

GRAY: The climax came when he put it on the basis that

if he couldn't see the project through to fruition, then he didn't want to stay with the company. So it became for us a question of going ahead with a program we didn't believe in or losing the man, who was brilliant and very valuable. We chose to let the man go. To this day, thulium is not a commercially practical isotope for x-rays. It just struck out completely and cesium has most of the market.

In one sense, that was a kind of easy decision, at least so far as the thulium program went. You just decided it was commercially hopeless. But what about the case where there is some commercial potential. Do you have any rigorous standards for deciding how much potential you require before you go ahead?

ASH: It can't really be standardized. I don't think a formula can ever govern the kinds of decisions that have to be made in this area. We look for and expect a potential that's worthy of the size and risk of the investment. I must say, what's worthy is a highly subjective matter.

Do you ever consciously play long shots, on the basis that if they come in there'll be a big payoff?

ASH: In a sense, our entry into inertial navigation was a long shot. Today, we're the acknowledged leader in that field, and it represents about $200 million of business—more than any other activity we're in. But when we started in 1954, many others were in the field, and we had nothing except a new technical concept. Anyway, we made a very big investment relative to our size at the time, and the engineers developing the system kept going around the clock for three or four years. If you'd seen that tremendous dedication to succeed, maybe you wouldn't have rated this a long shot. But an outsider would certainly have said it was at least ten to one against us, and some of our competitors did say that. I guess I really can't think of any cases where we deliberately went into something telling ourselves that the odds were ten to one. You know, I don't think there are many of those long shots in business that make sense; you don't find many successes where the payoff is so tremendous that you should take that kind of risk.

And there hasn't been any tendency to take more chances as you got bigger?

GRAY: Do you mean appropriating money as though we could afford to throw it away? We'd never do that.

Well, on the basis that you can afford to lose more often because you have more bets going.

ASH: It's true that as we've grown larger we've been able to undertake more development programs simultaneously, and of course not every one succeeds. But we count heavily on maintaining a good batting average.

Changing the subject, you spend a lot of time telling your story in the investment community, don't you?

GRAY: No, the fact is that we turn down a lot of invitations to make presentations to the security analysts.

ASH: I spoke to the New York analysts this year, and Tex did about two years ago, but those are the only two times in our history we've been there. Anyway, there's no need for us to go looking for interested investors—the security analysts keep coming to us.

Your annual reports are extraordinary—as though you wanted to make a particular mark with investors.

ASH: Well, there are some reasons for that. We've been undertaking a lot of new and different activities in fairly rapid order, and so we can use the annual reports to tell the public about them in great detail. Now the public believes it understands the products and work of most billion-dollar companies. It may not really know them, but it thinks it does. With Litton, they don't even *think* they know—so we like to help them get acquainted. That's the first reason. The second reason is that we don't do much institutional advertising. We've been spending only about $50,000 a year on institutional advertising, and you'll have to agree that's very little for a billion-dollar company. So our annual report serves some of the same function. Our salesmen use it. Of course, we do product advertising.

About this problem that people don't have Litton in focus

—do you flinch when someone refers to the company as a "conglomerate"?

ASH: Yes, I don't think it fits.

Well, what should you be called?

ASH: I'm not sure that the company fits into any of the usual classifications. Our own concept is that we're a technological company—I know that isn't sufficiently descriptive for most people—and that our business is to take the many different technologies of today and find ways of using them to develop commercially useful products. So we're a multi-industry company.

As a technological company, what would you do if you saw a chance to make a very high return on your investment in a nontechnological area?

ASH: We have declined many opportunities to make such investments. So far, technology is the common denominator of just about all the things we do—or plan to do.

Well, why do you resist a proposition that is not technological but is clearly profitable?

ASH: Because we are trying to build a company that is meaningful as a whole—that rests upon a coherent relationship between its different parts.

GRAY: A few years ago, we were interested in buying a subsidiary of a brewing company—the subsidiary was doing some advanced work in ceramics technically related to one of our fields. When we looked into it further, we found there was a possibility that we could buy the whole company, but we couldn't buy the subsidiary alone. So we called it off, because we're not interested in brewing.

ASH: We couldn't add anything to that business. Where we've entered so far, we like to think that we've been able to achieve—to use an overworked word—a synergistic effect.

Another way of putting it, then, would be that you're not interested in the commercial application where there's no science or technology.

ASH: Well, I would agree.

How does your recent interest in the Job Corps fit into the over-all Litton concept?

Ash: Over the years, in our military work we have developed a systems management capability and are interested in using it in new ways. This is clearly just a first step. Twenty years from now, looking backward, we may say that the really significant fallout from the defense business has been the development of the systems management concept of tackling major problems. We think this concept has tremendous potential and many applications. You can think of it as a new kind of technology itself. The solution to the country's problems of urban renewal, for example, will depend on an ability to approach those problems the way government and industry approached some of the military and space tasks.

Gray: When you get into the social sciences, the problems are tougher—you're dealing with infinitely more variables than in the physical sciences.

Ash: We think our country will be better off if there's a heavy involvement of private industry in these public-sector programs. We plan to be in a number of them—economic development, solving water-resources problems, and developing new cities.

What's your potential role in developing cities? Are you really going to be involved in creating new cities from the ground up?

Ash: The *de novo* city is a very exciting concept. We all know the attention given to those tremendous problems of urban living today. In trying to find solutions, we've been hitting our heads against the wall; there just seem to be too many problems, and we can't solve any of them because they're all interrelated. Now maybe this is one of those situations in which the solution lies in integrating the problem and raising it to a higher level.

And the "higher level" is the de novo *city?*

Ash: That's right; instead of trying to accommodate ten million more people a year in our present cities—and that's how many more we'll have each year toward the end of this century—we'll create new cities. All you have to do is fly over the country to see square mile after square mile where you could quite well set down a whole new city. There's no reason why you can't take 200 square miles some place that has the natural resources, which means primarily water—and even the water problem can be solved separately if it has to be—and create an ideal city with solutions for all these urban problems before it's even built.

How big a city are we talking about?
ASH: By 1970 we think that we'll be able to build a city that is adequate for 25,000 and has prospects of growing to 500,000. By 1990 we will be designing cities for a million people with the prospect of growing to five million.

It sounds fascinating, but where is the technological spin on this? You're not just going to end up in the real-estate business, are you?
ASH: Don't worry about that. The systems management work involved in getting a one-million-population city in business overnight is probably more sophisticated, and requires more professional disciplines, than the work required to get to the moon. When we decided to go to the moon, we found we had to create new kinds of professional capabilities—specializations that hadn't even existed. I think that the *de novo* city will lead to an entire new wave of specializations.

At what stage is your work on this now?
ASH: We're still studying and talking.

This new deal you've been working on with the Greek Government, to help develop Crete and the western Peloponnesus, and to build up parts of the country as tourist attractions—how did that originate?
ASH: Our man in Brussels, Pierre Guillaume, had been interested in this economic development concept, and he ran into a member of the Greek Government—I think they happened to meet in Zurich—who'd been thinking along the same lines, that is, of applying private management capabilities to some of these public problems. We got a feasibility contract just to see what might be done, and we completed

that a year ago. Now we're negotiating the development contract itself.

How about your new involvement in economic development in the Middle East—your participation in this United Banking & Investment Corp.?

ASH: That's a quite different proposition. First of all, there's no managerial role, as there is in Greece. The object of United Banking is to finance projects in the Middle East. Some of the projects may be related to our special capabilities, and ultimately we may develop a managerial role in them; but for now, we're simply one of several companies providing investment capital. The others are Western Bancorporation and three Arab banking groups. This venture is an entirely new departure for Litton, and it's hard to say now just what it might lead to.

In 1963, Tex Thornton was quoted as saying that "the best story on Litton will be done three years from now, when the things that are cooking today will be visible." What was he thinking of?

ASH: Expanding our business-equipment activities was very much on our minds then, and as you know we've since acquired Royal McBee, got into office-copying equipment, and built up Monroe Sweda considerably. When we took over Sweda, they'd established a beachhead in the cash-register business—but only a beachhead. Now a beachhead isn't a position to maintain permanently, in business or in war. You either go inland or you get out. We were resolved to go inland, and we've succeeded to a considerable extent. We're a major supplier of complex military computers through our Data Systems Division, but in the commercial market our interest right now is in the software and peripheral equipment. We've been offering more and more of this since we acquired Mellonics.

Is it possible to develop a major position in software if you aren't offering the hardware too?

ASH: That's the question, all right. There are two views of the case: One side says that if you don't make the hardware yourself you can be more objective about the customer's requirements. The other side says that you may be more objective but you have less insight into the equipment's capabilities. However, it's still too early to say how this software market will develop.

Why are you in shipbuilding? That Ingalls acquisition in 1961 probably did more than any other single thing to confuse people about Litton's general direction.

ASH: We saw some developments coming and thought we could be a part of them. One thing we foresaw was an expansion of the practice—it was already established in the Air Force and for Navy aircraft—of turning to industry for help in developing total weapon systems. We didn't want to get into shipbuilding just to take someone else's designs and then weld steel plates to specifications. Once we got into shipbuilding, we saw another opportunity developing in containerized shipping, specially designed cargo ships based on the efficiency of containerization. There's still a tremendous potential in the U.S. for ship improvements through new technology. We can't continue to excuse our inability to compete in world markets by saying we have high labor costs in our shipyards. U.S. aircraft companies compete with countries that have lower labor costs, but they beat out other countries' planes.

Was there much debate within your organization about taking on Ingalls?

ASH: It was fairly strenuous. When they first came to us with Ingalls, we almost said no without really considering it carefully. But then we decided to look into it.

What was the conclusive argument for the deal?

ASH: In addition to the special opportunities I've mentioned, we felt that the economics weren't too risky—that we could recover our purchase price in ten years even if the new developments were slower than we hoped.

How do your deals usually originate? Do they come to you or do you search them out?

ASH: Most of the ones that work out are acquisitions we've sought. At any one time, we're probably pursuing a number

of different ones. Some of them we never get and some of them take years. But a lot of other deals do come in to us—how many would you say, two a day, three a day?
GRAY: At least.

These are serious proposals?
ASH: Most of them aren't very serious. All kinds of outside sources drop names in the hopper, and ninety-five out of a hundred we drop right back out of the hopper.

How many deals in a year might you get to the stage of considering seriously? Fifty?
GRAY: Fifty's a pretty good estimate.

What are some other areas you're interested in expanding into now?
ASH: One is this business of automatic revenue collection, for subway and bus systems particularly. Today that's less than one-half of 1 percent of our business, which means it's less than $5 million, but we're counting on some growth there into the mid-millions, that is, between $10 million and $100 million.
GRAY: Another is the computer-controlled warehouse. Then there's materials handling generally. Also, this whole business of military command-and-control systems has considerable potential. Then there are consumer products we plan to be in. There has been a lot of outside speculation as to our possible interest in some consumer lines, and it's a fact that we have some ideas.

As you get into more and more new fields, do you have any sense of increased antitrust problems?
ASH: We're aware of antitrust considerations in everything we do, and I think we've done a good job of keeping well within the rules. In retrospect, I think we've generally been on the side of the Justice Department because we've so often been the challenger in a field where someone else had a dominant position.

Has the Justice Department or the FTC gone after you at all?

Ash: On three occasions they've asked us to fill out the customary forms and supply information. On two of those, we supplied what they wanted and they said fine, no problems. On the third, we haven't heard from them yet but we believe we've satisfied them.

Let's get back to your stock. For a company your size you're close to being unique, aren't you, in refusing to pay a cash dividend on your common stock?

Ash: I think investors are in Litton because they expect growth. Investors who want income have many other companies to choose among.

Can you tell us about the concept of the new Litton "preference stock"? Wall Street's been terribly confused about the concept, and about the terms themselves.

Ash: We're appealing here to an investor who wants all the good features of the classical securities and none of the bad ones. The investor gets a choice between a cash return and holding out for growth. If he holds the preference stock, it becomes convertible into an increasing number of common shares each year—the number rises by 3 percent a year. Alternatively, he can sell 3 percent of the preference stock each year and still have conversion rights to his original number of common shares. Finally, there's a safety feature: whatever happens to the common, we offer to redeem 3 percent of the preference stock annually at a price that rises every year—again, by 3 percent.

Whose idea was it?

Ash: It was created by a number of us together. And I think the issue demonstrates that there are still opportunities to bring some new ideas into a field that's generally followed certain traditions.

It sounds as though your persistent originality about all sorts of matters must create conflicts for you in other fields that have strong traditions—conflicts with bankers, lawyers, actuaries, and so on.

Ash: Well, we have tried to solve that problem by creating these services in-house. We have our own law organization— lawyers who have a close understanding of our business and

our objectives. Their job isn't just to sit around telling us all
the things we can't do.

*Sounds as though you'd like to do your own public ac-
counting.*

ASH: We can't do that, of course. We have Touche, Ross,
who've been with us from the beginning. Our accounting is
very conservative, by the way. We don't capitalize R. and D.
costs. We amortize our capital assets just as rapidly as possible. We don't take all the investment credit in one year;
we spread it out. In the business-equipment field, all our
field inventories of parts are written down to zero. Revenues
on maintenance contracts for business equipment are taken
into income over the life of the contract—not as soon as
they're received.

What's your accounting bill these days?

GRAY: About $200,000 a year for the regular audit, but
there are special jobs too.

In connection with your acquisitions?

GRAY: That's right. Our own internal auditors do a thorough review of any acquisition while the deal is pending.
But when more than one big deal at a time is pending—
an extreme case was in 1964, when we were negotiating for
both Royal McBee and Hewitt-Robins—we'll ask Touche,
Ross to do a special job for us.

Have these audits ever led to a deal being torpedoed?

GRAY: Oh, yes. Our auditors have told us that the other
company's representations were not what they'd been held
to be. When we start negotiating, we don't ask a company
to open up all its books to us right away—you can't expect
that when nobody knows if the deal is likely—but we do ask
for representations about certain critical matters, so that
we'll have a fair notion about the values involved and the
price we might be willing to pay. If the representations then
prove to be incorrect, either the price gets changed or the
deal is off.

How big is your own internal auditing operation?

GRAY: We have eighteen C.P.A.s on our staff. In California, you know, before anyone can be certified as a public accountant he has to pass the exam and also get some practical experience—which almost always means working for one of the public accounting firms. But he can also get his practical-experience qualification if he works in Litton's auditing department. The state recognizes it as the equivalent of a C.P.A. firm for that purpose.

Do your auditors work on anything aside from acquisitions?

GRAY: They also keep management on top of any operating problems in our own divisions. We audit them continuously, so that we'll know about problems right away, when there's time to do something about them—we don't want to get clobbered by some big year-end adjustment. So a lot of the Touche, Ross audit really duplicates work we've done ourselves.

We've been roaming over a pretty wide range. Is there any large and obvious point about Litton that we've forgotten to mention?

ASH: There's one point that may be taken too much for granted. It's about our people. This is a "people business," and talking just about products and markets and research overlooks that point. Every business is a people business in some sense, of course, but we think we've brought together some particular kinds of people and provided them with a very special environment. Our kind of man is the kind you usually think of as an entrepreneur—he thinks and acts as though he's in business for himself. Most of our executives would be if they weren't here at Litton. They're highly motivated people.

When you talk about entrepreneurs, how many people are you referring to?

ASH: Well, first, the division managers—there are more than forty executives right there. But if you mean all the people who approach their responsibilities like entrepreneurs, the number would probably be closer to a thousand.

Actually, some people have left Litton to go into business for themselves, and they've done remarkably well. Teledyne was started by your people and Walter Kidde was pretty much transformed by some other Litton people. Tell us a bit more about your environment.

ASH: We have a level of enthusiasm in the company we don't want to lose. In some organizations, where a man's ideas are knocked down once or twice, he's not apt to come up with a third one. We try to sustain an atmosphere in which every idea is a good idea—unless proven otherwise. We want people to keep throwing in all the ideas they have.

Still, I'd imagine that the Litton environment must look kind of scary to some people on the outside—people whose companies you want to acquire, say.

ASH: Well, we can understand that not everybody wants to get into this kind of environment. I know we have scared some who may feel the pace of Litton is different from what they're used to.

I gather from the remarks about all your entrepreneurs that you view Litton as a collection of related small companies rather than as one large one.

ASH: That's right, and it gets back to your original question—about how we keep on growing when we don't have some big lock on a new technology or market. If, in fact, you look at Litton, not as a $1-billion company, but as a number of $10-million to $100-million companies, then you might see that we have a large number of individually strong positions. We're not totally dependent on any one field, but we have a lot of different capabilities.

Gulf & Western's Rambunctious Conservatism

EVEN THOSE WHO HAD BEEN closely watching its cometlike course were startled this winter when Gulf & Western Industries announced its intention to acquire Armour & Co., a company whose sales last year were three times its own and a famous name in American business for a century. Though talks with Armour were suspended after three breathless weeks, Gulf & Western was almost simultaneously involved in a flurry of other Brobdingnagian deals. It swallowed up E. W. Bliss, Universal American, and Consolidated Cigar, whose combined sales exceed $500 million a year, and disclosed plans to buy all or part of four other companies with revenues above $350 million.

Wall Street was not completely awed. Gulf & Western's latest acquisition spree came at a time of rising concern about the viability of such rapidly expanding conglomerates. The nervousness was intensified by the news that Litton Industries, long judged to be the most firmly based of these "multi-market" corporations, had "substantially lower" earnings for the quarter ended January 31 than for the comparable period a year earlier—and was blaming the decline, not on the vagaries of the economy, but on "earlier deficiencies of management personnel." It was a heart-warming day for skeptics who have recurrently contended that the con-

44

glomerates cannot sustain their fast growth rates, that they have undertaken a management task beyond human capability, that they inflate their reported earnings by promotional tricks with their accounting. The worries penetrated to where they counted most, among the institutional investors. Howard Stein, president of the Dreyfus Fund, warned, "Whether the conglomerates have long-term staying power is something we should be concerned about."

A Perch on a Himalayan Curve

As nearly everybody knows now, conglomerates embody something quite new in the saga of capitalism. With their insouciance about debt, their unique approach to maximizing their shareholders' return, and their readiness to plunge into almost any industry provided they can get the right terms and the right people, they are raising basic questions about the nature of business and the purpose of corporations. In the process, they are tacitly challenging the wisdom, and even the competence of corporations that cling to the old structural forms.

So it is not surprising that many businessmen and investors remain unconvinced. As a group, the conglomerates have yet to show that they can weather even a moderate general recession; many of them are so new that it is still too early to make final judgments on how well they can manage what they have so hastily acquired.

Gulf & Western has evoked even more than its share of wariness. Though its annual gains in sales and earnings have led the major conglomerates, the price-earnings ratio on its stock has consistently been the lowest. The impression has spread that its broad-ranging acquisition program conforms to no logical plan. Litton, by contrast, is widely identified with the development and application of advanced technology, and I.T.T. with the imposition on diverse companies of tightly centralized modern management. Gulf & Western has often appeared to be seizing any company it could get its hands on in a headlong scramble for growth. If any pattern is discernible, it has seemed to be a preference for prosaic companies in prosaic industries: auto parts, zinc mining, motion pictures, cigars, meatpacking. Finally, the company has to contend with a prevalent suspicion that Charles G. Bluhdorn, its Austrian-born chairman, is something of a gauche immigrant boy on the make.

Some of the reservations about Gulf & Western are justified. A downturn in earnings or an enforced pause in its acquisition program could do severe harm to any company that is so daringly perched on a Himalayan growth curve. But Gulf & Western is no jerry-built structure. Its expansion has been guided by some surprisingly conservative principles that make it potentially more resistant to economic reverses than many other conglomerates.

In choosing acquisitions, all conglomerates have an instinct for the main chance, and all are good at rationalizing opportunistic purchases after the fact. However, Gulf & Western has pretty consistently chosen companies with impressive and underutilized tangible assets. It has also quite consciously sought to enter industries that are either intrinsically noncyclical, such as auto parts, or that can reasonably be expected not to go down simultaneously—mining and movies, for example. "We're like an investment company," said Bluhdorn, "except that they just sit upstairs and watch the horses run. We get down and manage the horses."

The predilection for hard assets and stability—reinforced by its own relatively low p/e ratio—has kept Gulf & Western's interest focused mainly on well-established companies in conventional industries. The conviction behind its strategy is that these companies will do better under its wing than they did operating independently. The measurement of success by this standard gets into difficult intangibles. But there is one revealing indicator: the internal growth of Gulf & Western's net earnings, stripped of the year-to-year gains

---

The Fine Art of Buying Sales

As it acquires bigger and bigger companies, Gulf & Western's sales curve zooms ever more steeply. The chart traces the company's reported sales through fiscal 1967. The figure for 1968 is the company's estimate; the estimated $650-million increase reflects the impact of six recent mergers, including those with South Puerto Rico Sugar and Taylor Forge, which were completed late in fiscal 1967.

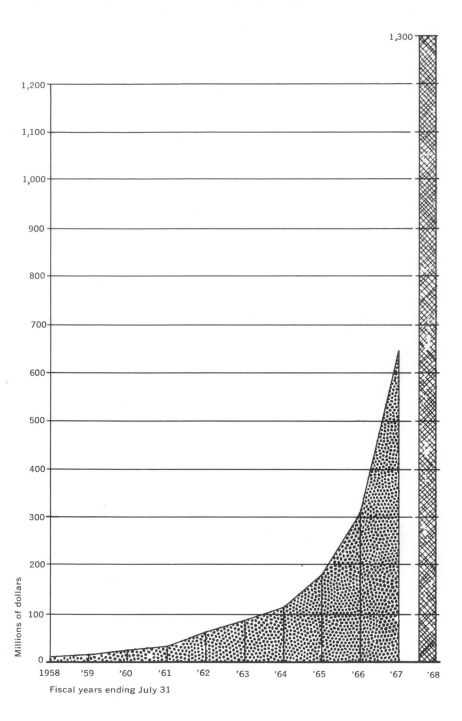

Millions of dollars

1,300
1,200
1,100
1,000
900
800
700
600
500
400
300
200
100
0

1958 '59 '60 '61 '62 '63 '64 '65 '66 '67 '68

Fiscal years ending July 31

produced by acquisitions, has averaged above 18 percent annually.

Though the company has been enlarging its financial and internal management-consulting staffs, there are still only ninety-five people (including secretaries) working at Gulf & Western's blue-carpeted headquarters on Madison Avenue. Major policy decisions remain in the hands of a half-dozen top officers, who together control about 10 percent of the company's stock. They make up one of the most cosmopolitan managerial teams in American business. The core of the group is the triumvirate of Bluhdorn, President David N. Judelson, and executive-committee chairman John H. Duncan. They have been working together since 1957, when Bluhdorn gained control of Michigan Bumper, an auto-parts manufacturer that became the nucleus of Gulf & Western.

Charles Bluhdorn, brash, excitable, and full of fire, is, as he has always been, the dominant figure. The memories of his early hair-raising capers in the commodity market, which made him a millionaire in his mid-twenties, still live with him. "Today, when I have the means to do it, I wouldn't have the nerve," he says. Now forty-one, Bluhdorn still fights to put down the popular suspicion that the main difference between his business today and fifteen years ago is that the commodities to be traded now are corporations instead of bags of coffee. "How can anyone wheel and deal with a New Jersey Zinc?" he asks. "Or a South Puerto Rico Sugar or a Paramount? It's absolutely impossible. We have a rogues' gallery of conservatism in Gulf & Western."

An outsider confronted with Bluhdorn for the first time has no difficulty imagining him as the *enfant terrible* of the commodity exchange. He delights in the scale of his dealings. His manner changes swiftly from persuasive explanation to table-thumping assertion, all enunciated in mile-a-minute Viennese-American. His single-mindedness about the rightness and logic of his mission in the business world can display itself in rudeness and irascibility as well as in sudden charm. And yet in many of his associates, including the heads of some of the companies that at first resisted Gulf & Western's advances, he inspires an admiration that borders on love. Says Lindsay Johnson, president of New Jersey Zinc, which Gulf & Western acquired in 1966: "The more you're around Bluhdorn, the closer the moon is."

David Judelson, thirty-nine, who is invariably called by his childhood nickname Jim, supervises the operating divisions. He is a short, intense, neatly tailored graduate of New York University's engineering school, who once ran his father's machinery company in Jersey City. John Duncan, forty, is a folksy, soft-spoken Texan, who was helping to manage his family's coffee company in Houston when he first met Bluhdorn. He guided the development of Gulf & Western's $100-million auto-parts distribution system. Duncan became president of the corporation in 1959, but resigned last year because he preferred to stay in Texas when the head office was moved from Houston to New York. As chairman of the executive committee, he continues to coordinate the company's long-term planning.

Since the beginning, Gulf & Western's legal affairs have been handled by its secretary and general counsel, Joel Dolkart, fifty-one, a partner in the New York law firm of Simpson, Thacher & Bartlett and an authority on the legal problems involved in take-overs. Two shrewd young financial officers have more recently signed on: Executive Vice President Don F. Gaston, a thirty-three-year-old Texas accountant hired away from Ernst & Ernst, and Senior Vice President Roy T. Abbott Jr., thirty-seven, who was a vice president of Chase Manhattan Bank.

Expertise from Seventy-Two Mergers

The managers of a large conglomerate have to divide their daily attention between two related but distinctly separate lines of work: acquisition and operation. Because so much of their capital is committed to acquisitions, all the top executives need a sure grasp of financial matters and an ability to pass judgment on merger prospects. Gulf & Western has evolved a Litton-like management system based on decentralized operations with centralized financial controls. Most of the newly acquired subsidiaries are still run by the same men who were in charge before Gulf & Western took over. Bluhdorn's headquarters team has been enviably proficient at keeping alive, and indeed heightening, the entrepreneurial zeal of these executives without getting bogged down itself in the day-to-day problems of the subsidiaries.

Gulf & Western makes its distinctive mark in the business of acquisition. Says Joel Dolkart: "After many acquisitions we've developed a *modus vivendi*, if you will, so we are able to do things others can't do." The expertise accumulated from carrying out seventy-two mergers displays itself in the speed with which the individual skills of all the top executives can be marshaled to assess a potential purchase, and their facility in the arcane verbal shorthand that summarizes the endless legal, tax, and financial questions involved in mergers. "I feel sorry for the company that has three acquisitions and then stops," says John Duncan. "If we're going to make a thousand mistakes in our corporate history, I feel we made half of them in our first three acquisitions."

The most fateful decisions in any acquisition program are those that determine which companies will be sought and which should be passed up. Gulf & Western executives dislike the word "conglomerate" because it connotes aimless accretion. They insist that there is nothing aimless about their acquisitions. But the company stands ready to adapt its plan when something good becomes available unexpectedly. New Jersey Zinc, for example, was brought to Bluhdorn's attention in 1965, when Gulf & Western was still almost exclusively in the auto-parts business. The go-between was Harold U. Zerbe, who was a director of both companies. The zinc company had a lot of cash, and was arguing about what to do with it. Management wanted to expand operations; the group of controlling owners, led by Jacob L. Hain, chairman of Bush Terminal Co., wanted to enlarge New Jersey Zinc's investment portfolio. Gulf & Western took management's side and within days after serious negotiations started was able to borrow $84 million from Chase Manhattan Bank to buy the Hain group's 57.5 percent interest.

Jim Judelson visualizes Gulf & Western as a wheel, with parent management at the hub and the spokes representing the various loosely defined operating areas: manufacturing, distribution, "leisure time," consumer products, metals and chemicals, and agriculture. When a major acquisition is made in one area, that spoke is thickened. In order to prevent the company from becoming overdependent on any one industry, it becomes necessary to enlarge the other spokes or add new ones.

This is a pat rationale for unending expansion, but it does provide some insight into how Gulf & Western begins to cull promising acquisitions out of hundreds of possibilities. Piles of sale offers cross Bluhdorn's and Judelson's desks every week. For every take-over it completes, the company looks at fifty or sixty prospects. Even after the stage of preliminary negotiation is reached, about four out of five deals fall through, often because of disagreement over terms.

With its compact central management, Gulf & Western must avoid becoming a hospital for sick companies. It looks for companies that are important factors in growing industries and that have capable managers who would stay at their desks if Gulf & Western took over. Such companies are always in comparatively short supply, and many obviously have no interest in being bought. The reluctance may quickly melt, however, if the terms are right. And the offering price often demonstrates that Gulf & Western takes a more optimistic view of a company's potential than its owners do.

To maintain growth in per-share earnings, Gulf & Western figures that new acquisitions must promise at least a 10 to 12 percent return on its investment. It cannot make a practice of buying companies whose price-earnings ratios are substantially higher than its own. This restriction makes Gulf & Western executives wistful; they like to point out that companies with high p/e ratios have much wider scope. "Do you realize," says one officer, "that Xerox, with its multiple, could sell common stock, put the money in Treasury bills, and still increase its per-share earnings?"

But Judelson believes that the discipline has been good for Gulf & Western. He cites with indignation a deal in which another large conglomerate, using its high-ratio stock, paid thirty-three times earnings and four times book value for an acquisition. "This company will not do that as long as I'm around," he insists, "because I know how hard it is to produce a dollar of earnings and I know what it's worth."

Once Bluhdorn and Judelson have decided what kind of price they might pay, they get in touch with the prospect to see if there is a basis for negotiations. (Gulf & Western may also buy a little of the prospect's stock on the side, just to establish a foothold.*) If they receive even the mildest encouragement, Gulf & Western's well-oiled acquisition machine springs into action. While Bluhdorn harangues the management and directors about the new world of excitement, challenge, and unimaginable growth that will unfold the minute they join Gulf & Western, other executives begin a more exhaustive investigation of the company's operations, finances, and markets.

If the analysis justifies Gulf & Western's original enthusiasm, hard bargaining over terms begins. By this time, Bluhdorn and Judelson have a pretty clear idea of the maximum they are willing to pay, but they can be extremely flexible about the means of payment. This can be as important an issue as the price itself; in fact, it can influence the price, since different forms of payment have different tax and accounting consequences.

Usually it is the seller who finally determines how payment will be made. Some companies insist on cash. Others will not accept it, because it could expose their owners to capital-gains taxes. If Gulf & Western offers securities in lieu of cash, its choices range from common shares, which offer potential capital gains but only token dividends, to debentures, with assured high interest payments but no growth. In between, there is a constellation of preferred stock, convertible preferred, warrants, and convertible debentures. If necessary, alternative options can be offered or a new issue can be created to provide just the required balance between risk and income.

A Penchant for Convertibles

When it has the chance to acquire assets at a favorable price, Gulf & Western may go ahead with a merger even if

---

* In addition to these corporate purchases, Bluhdorn himself has bought large blocks of stock in at least two companies that later were acquired by Gulf & Western: Paramount and South Puerto Rico Sugar. He sold the Paramount shares to Gulf & Western at his cost. He accepted a gain on the sale of the South Puerto Rico shares to Gulf & Western because, he says, he had purchased them jointly with a partner.

it doesn't promise any immediate boost to earnings. This fascination with assets has nothing to do with their liquidation value. Of all the companies acquired, only two small ones were later sold off, both more than five years ago. One reason Gulf & Western wants the assets is that it can borrow heavily against them and thus gain an important source of cash.

No aura of sin clings to the concept of debt at Gulf & Western. Leveraging capital with high borrowings is viewed as the obvious course of action for a company that wants to make maximum use of its assets. "Compare the price of anything twenty years ago and its price today," says Bluhdorn. "The best buy you can make today is to put out paper and know that twenty years from now you can pay out the same amount of money."

Many analysts accept Gulf & Western's rationale for debt. But some have been less willing to shrug off the company's recent penchant for issuing convertible securities. If converted into common stock, these would substantially reduce per-share earnings.

Gulf & Western has been issuing convertibles only since 1966. To its credit, it has disclosed the potential dilution threatened by the existence of these securities, as well as by warrants and stock options. And even with full allowance for dilution, earnings have been rising respectably, though not as dramatically as the undiluted figures.

In the fiscal year that ended July 31, 1965—just before the start of Gulf & Western's conglomerate phase—per-share earnings were 81 cents. (Figures have been adjusted for subsequent splits and stock dividends.) In fiscal 1966, bolstered by acquisitions, including New Jersey Zinc, they rose over 200 percent to $2.67. But potential dilution, previously negligible, jumped to about 23 percent in that year; thus, earnings after dilution would have been $2.05 a share. During fiscal 1967 there was little change in the amount of potential dilution, and both undiluted and diluted earnings rose over 40 percent—to $3.79 and $2.93, respectively.

With the acquisitions completed since last July, earnings are currently running at an estimated annual rate of around $5 per common share. But the $375 million of convertibles issued to acquire E. W. Bliss, Universal American, and Consolidated Cigar has increased potential dilution to about 37 percent. So if all outstanding convertibles, options, and warrants were traded for common, that $5 would fall to something like $3.15—or only 7.5 percent above last year's diluted figure.

Motorizing the Driftwood

The problems of managing a conglomerate are still new to Gulf & Western, because it has not, in fact, been a conglomerate for long. Between 1958, when its sales were $8,395,000, and fiscal 1965, when they reached $182,079,000, the company stayed close to the business of making and distributing auto parts. Bluhdorn had a clear concept for that chaotic industry; with dozens of acquisitions, Gulf & Western welded together a solid component-manufacturing complex and a distribution system streamlined by modern inventory controls. But the merger with New Jersey Zinc in February 1966 really marked Gulf & Western's emergence as a conglomerate.

To justify itself economically, a conglomerate must demonstrate ability to improve the performance of the companies it acquires. Gulf & Western's past record here is good, but it is still fair to question how well the company is handling the businesses it has acquired outside the auto-parts field. Most of these companies have been with Gulf & Western for less than two years (some much less), and it is unclear how much of the credit for their performance can legitimately be claimed by their new parent, though the portents are good.

Gulf & Western keeps close tabs on the financial affairs of all its units. Five-year goals are set for each one. Every three months, each division is required to forecast its sales, profit, cash flow, cash needs, and capital expenditures for the following five quarters. These forecasts are later checked against the monthly financial reports submitted by the divisions.

The company takes advantage of some administrative economies of scale—e. g., centralized tax accounting and insurance buying. It also acts as a bank for the operating units, which are discouraged from keeping more cash than they require for their most imminent expenses. The subsidiaries earn interest on even the shortest-term deposits they leave with the parent and, conversely, they pay interest on money they borrow. This constant movement of money ensures that the whole corporation can operate with much less cash than it would need if all the units were independent. It also quickly alerts management to units that are doing particularly well or badly.

In its dealings with subsidiaries, management can wield psychological as well as financial influence. "Nine-tenths of companies are driftwood," asserts Bluhdorn. "Our job is to motorize the driftwood." Gulf & Western encourages operating managers to consult informally with top executives. The heads of many subsidiaries are elated by the parent company's evident enthusiasm for fast development of their assets and its broad view of the possibilities open to them. Remarks Lindsay Johnson of New Jersey Zinc: "A lot of people say, 'Oh, too bad—an old, conservative company that used to be listed on the Exchange has been gobbled up.' I don't subscribe to that at all. An old, conservative company has been taken into a new, vital situation."

Perhaps the most dramatic and visible impact of Gulf & Western on a subsidiary can be found at Paramount Pictures, because there Charlie Bluhdorn himself is doing the moving and shaking. When Gulf & Western took charge in October 1966, Paramount was moribund. Like most big movie companies, it was suffering heavy losses on its feature-film productions. It had shied away from producing television programs, and was unsystematically leasing its old movies to the networks on comparatively disadvantageous terms. Paramount's accounts were kept by pen-wielding clerks in what was known as "the green-eyeshade department." Data on foreign rentals, which account for half the company's revenues on first-run films, often arrived weeks late at the head office. Paramount's elderly executives had been propping up earnings by selling off assets, including some TV stations and the Paramount Building on Times Square.

Bluhdorn's first major act after the $125-million take-over was to upend Paramount's management. He installed himself as president. Martin S. Davis, forty-one, who had been a vice president and director of advertising and public relations, became executive vice president and chief operating officer. Responsibility for foreign and domestic film productions was separated, and new men were put in charge. Paramount brought in James J. Burke, thirty-nine, who had been with Litton Industries, as financial vice president and treasurer, and Richard D. Spence, a twenty-nine-year-old lending officer for Chase Manhattan Bank, as vice president. Bluhdorn commandeered space for himself in a green-walled, chandeliered room adjoining Davis's New York office.

With Bluhdorn and Davis in charge, Paramount usually can decide in a day or two whether to invest in a film production; previously, some potentially lucrative projects evaporated while Paramount waited for a board of directors' vote, which often took weeks. Budgets for films, which used to be mostly hopeful guesses, now are worked out in such detail that the company can tell whether costs are awry in the first few days of shooting.

Paramount moved seriously into television production last year when Gulf & Western acquired control of Desilu Productions. It also stepped up the leasing of its feature films to television. Three major deals were made with A.B.C. and C.B.S., and films were syndicated to local stations for the first time. Rentals of films and series to television by Paramount and Desilu totaled $87,805,000 in fiscal 1967, up from $46,525,000 the year before.

For years, Paramount's studios and lots in Hollywood had been the expensive captive plant of its production staff; facilities were often idled for weeks by producers who wanted to keep them available for their own projects. By forcing each department to look after its own profit-and-loss statement, executives have been able to learn for the first time exactly which costs are attributable to productions and which to studio overhead. The change has spurred studio managers to market idle sound stages more aggressively to independent producers; Davis says the lots now are in use nearly all the time instead of only about a third of the time.

Possibly the saddest tale to emerge from Gulf & Western's upheaval of Paramount is what might be labeled the Funnies Fiasco. Paramount had long operated an animation studio on the West Side of Manhattan. Gulf & Western discovered that the cartoon business was earning back none of its $750,000 annual overhead and was not even covering its own shipping costs. Each time a theatre rented a cartoon, Paramount received an average payment of $2.80; the cost of shipping the film, sending a man to collect it at the station on its return, and entering the transaction in the ledger averaged over $15. Furthermore, the new management learned that most theatre owners don't like cartoons, because they cut down the number of times the feature can be shown each day and therefore reduce revenues. "It was a vicious cycle, and no one asked why," a Paramount man observes. Last year Paramount quietly closed down the cartoon studio.

Disquiet among the Accountants

Gulf & Western's relationship with Paramount has been seized upon by those who believe that the parent company is somehow juggling its accounts to produce splashy annual gains in profit. These critics complain about Gulf & Western's practice of recording the total value of Paramount's TV leases as income in the year the leases are signed, rather than waiting for the money actually to arrive. However, this method of accounting for installment leases was used by Paramount before Gulf & Western acquired it and is, in fact, followed by most major movie companies.

A broader criticism of Gulf & Western's accounting is the allegation that it understates the true costs of some acquisitions by accounting for them as "poolings of interests" rather than as purchases. Pooling of interests is permissible only in mergers effected through an exchange of voting stock. The principal objection to it is that when a company is acquired for more than its book value, as is usually the case, the parent corporation's balance sheet takes no account of the excess cost. In a straight purchase transaction, by contrast, the difference between book value and purchase price would show up on the balance sheet as a writing-up of assets or as "good will," either of which would probably have to be amortized against earnings eventually.

Furthermore, in pooling transactions, the sales and earnings of companies acquired are consolidated with those of the parent for all past periods covered in its financial statements. When a merger is completed at the end of a fiscal year, this artificially inflates the reported results for that year, making it harder for the parent company to show continued growth without further acquisitions the following year.

Pooling of interests is the subject of controversy among auditors, and learned articles pro and con appear in accounting journals. But the method is regularly used by nearly all companies that make a lot of acquisitions, and the Accounting Principles Board of the American Institute of Certified Public Accountants is trying to decide whether to recommend any change in the rules. Auditors who support the method maintain that it would be misleading to record the creation of a new asset in a transaction in which all parties end up holding stock in the merged corporation and no new cash has been invested in either company.

For its part, Gulf & Western says that whether acquisitions have been made above, below, or at book value, it has consistently accounted for them as poolings of interests when voting stock was exchanged, and as purchases when stock was not exchanged. It is pointless, the company argues, to ask what earnings would be today if pooling had never been permitted, because if the rules had been different, the deals would have been different.

Whether or not negotiations with Armour are eventually reopened, there is little likelihood that the pace or size of Gulf & Western's acquisitions will diminish. It has been looking hungrily at companies in industries including publishing, some branches of technology, consumer products, and transportation.

Some Inside Springboards

There is, however, increased interest among executives in entering new fields through internal expansion, partly because the company is reaching a sales level where acquisitions in any of several fields could cause antitrust problems. In the past, Gulf & Western has tried to avoid purchases that might raise antitrust questions. It did seek and receive favorable opinions from the Justice Department before buying New Jersey Zinc and Desilu. To win approval of the Desilu merger, Gulf & Western agreed to offer to sell off all but one of the TV company's production lots; it almost certainly will steer clear of further mergers in the film business.

The bid for Armour was suspended after a thirteen-point drop in the price of Gulf & Western stock. But antitrust problems also figured in the decision. A 1920 consent decree limiting the businesses that a meatpacker can own might have required Gulf & Western to spin off its sugar and cigar operations if it had taken over Armour. And there were indications that the Justice Department was thinking of making the combination a test case to challenge the legality of conglomerate mergers in general.

Gulf & Western has enormous springboards for internal diversification. Through such subsidiaries as Paramount, New Jersey Zinc, and South Puerto Rico Sugar (whose properties include 275,000 acres in the Dominican Republic), the company is a major landowner. It has active plans to develop its acreage for industrial and agricultural use and tourism. Using the patents and technical staff of a Paramount subsidiary, Gulf & Western hopes to develop a network of community-antenna television systems over three years at 10 percent of the cost of acquiring a comparable established operation. The company would also like to expand its European movie-making and auto-parts businesses, and perhaps make some new acquisitions in Europe.

If the day ever arrives when antitrust action or the vagaries of the stock market force Gulf & Western to curtail its acquisition program, Bluhdorn says he will be unfazed. "The biggest fun I'm getting is building a company—Paramount—without acquisitions," he insists. "When we have a big enough base, we can grow nicely on it. When the economy is bad, we'll get hit like anyone else. But we think we can always stay ahead because we have the people and the companies and can sit down at the table and say we'll do this and this. If the sugar business is bad, maybe we'll take some TV revenues and put them in sugar."

Any slowdown in Gulf & Western's almost geometric annual growth rates could, of course, touch off a spiral of even lower prices for its stock and hence ever-greater difficulties in making mergers. But it is already a formidable corporation. The signs that it is revitalizing newer subsidiaries like

Paramount and New Jersey Zinc, while still inconclusive, are promising. They lend credence to the belief that, even without continual acquisitions, Gulf & Western could perform well by any conventional standard. And in the sales league in which it is now operating, even plain old arithmetical growth can be distinctly impressive.

W. R. Grace Is Still Looking for That Magic

FOR A COMPANY that began to diversify when the word conglomerate was reserved for curious rock formations, and has pulled through any number of recessions and depressions with a near flawless dividend record, the firm of W. R. Grace & Co. has been taking quite a buffeting. The year 1969 opened inauspiciously with a national dock strike, idling ships of the Grace Line, which in other days propelled the family Grace to fame and fortune. In Latin America, Peru's military junta seized Grace's sugar properties and threatened its manufacturing facilities. Meanwhile, at home, Grace did nothing to improve its image as a consistent diversifier when it announced it was pulling out of Miller Brewing Co., which Grace's own 1968 corporate report had touted as a sparkling symbol of its aggressive investment program. Along Wall Street it is conceded that Grace management may know what it is doing, but as one of the shrewder investment bankers put it recently: "I just can't think of a situation which would interest us less at the present time."

Yet if one journeys down to No. 7 Hanover Square, where J. Peter Grace, third-generation head of this enormous enterprise, still maintains headquarters amidst the clang and clatter of Manhattan's changing financial district, some of the events of 1969 fall into perspective. In a matter of weeks, if all goes well, Grace will have completed the sale of the Grace Line to the Spyros P. Skouras interests, and so will be rid of what in recent years has proved itself to be a highly erratic earning property. Grace has taken a shellacking in Peru but its investment there now runs to about 10 percent of its $600-million net worth and a smaller fraction of its $1.7-billion sales. What has really pulled down Grace earnings from their bright record of the early sixties has been its hefty investment in agricultural fertilizers, where the giants of oil have contributed to a chronic condition of overproduction and overcapacity. Yet there are some signs that fertilizer prices have at least bottomed out, and should they turn around, Grace profits could bounce back handsomely. Meanwhile, sales of nonagricultural chemicals, which contribute about a third of Grace's sales and a much larger proportion of its profits, have been doing very well indeed.

More important, Peter Grace and his associates who manage this restless empire now find themselves in a strategic and enviable position to aim at new targets of opportunity. This is so not only because Grace is pulling out of the shipping business, but because of its controversial sale of Miller Brewing, which tells a good deal about the investment philosophy of this tough old company. Grace is not in the business of just investing money. It is in the far more difficult business of buying and, if need be, selling companies; and what Grace buys, it prefers to control and to manage. As we shall presently see in more detail, when Grace bought its 53-percent interest in Miller in 1966 for $36 million, it was confident that it could acquire the remaining 47 percent of the stock, and it worked assiduously to do so. It was only when this proved impossible that Grace looked for possible purchasers, first negotiating with PepsiCo and later with Philip Morris. When the latter company came up with a clean offer of $130 million in cash, Grace leapt at the opportunity, clearing a profit of $67 million after taxes. If that is not good business, implies Peter Grace, tipping back his glasses on a balding head, then what in the world is?

The crucial fact is that, with the sale of Miller plus

other divestitures made or to come, Grace fronts the future with some $150 million to $200 million in the till when such money is not exactly easy to come by. The fundamental problem is something more than one might grasp by casually reading the newspapers. It is certainly to increase earnings from their present lackluster estate to higher returns on sales and capital already sunk in the business. But it is also to find profitable outlets for all that newly gained liquidity in the big, clamorous, and ever-changing world of modern industry. At a time when all corporate managers are having to pay increasing attention to the deployment and redeployment of capital, W. R. Grace offers a kind of window for seeing that process at work over many years. It is a problem to which Peter Grace is giving plenty of attention as he works in his office in Hanover Square, or flits across the country in his JetStar, or makes his darting trips to Europe and the Far East. A man, he reflected recently, is given only so many chances to make good. This could be his big opportunity or it could be, as he puts it, "my last hurrah."

Which it will be remains to be decided, and Peter Grace starts the game with a complicated hand. For while W. R. Grace & Co. is a conglomerate in fact if not in name, it has grown to its present girth not by huge and sudden acquisitions, but by an organic process involving relatively small accretions. The result is a curious mosaic of enterprises not easily controlled or managed, and sometimes a bit baffling to Grace's own spokesmen. W. R. Grace today is a complex made up of fertilizer plants in Tennessee, and in Trinidad; industrial chemical companies scattered from Massachusetts to South Carolina to Kentucky to California; chocolate factories in Milwaukee and Koog Zaandijk in Holland; a share in oil concessions in troubled Libya; a Wisconsin farm devoted to improving cattle herds by artificial insemination; plus snack bars and restaurants along the expressways of Europe.

Yet if one turns to the figures of which Peter Grace is exceedingly fond (an adding machine stands ever at hand in his office), it is not too hard to impose a certain degree of order on this variegated assortment of investments. In 1968 W. R. Grace grossed $1.7 billion, of which 35 percent came from industrial chemicals of one kind or another, 20 percent from agricultural products (mostly fertilizers), and 26 percent from foods and so-called services. The remaining 19 percent of Grace's business came from steamship operations—which will probably drop out of the picture next year when the Grace Line is finally sold—petroleum production, papermaking (concentrated in Latin America), and what Grace accountants in sheer desperation label "other activities."

This agglomeration of enterprises has certainly grown, and in the past ten years Grace sales have about quadrupled and its net worth has better than doubled. When it comes to profits, the record is more spotty and more complicated, precisely because Grace is constantly acquiring companies while selling others. In 1968, for instance, some of the hand-wringing about Grace earnings was due to the fact that it took a bookkeeping loss of $32 million on the sale of the Grace Line (even though the sale of the property had not yet cleared the Maritime Commission). This pulled down final net earnings to $33 million, which ranked Grace close to the bottom of *Fortune*'s 500 list in return on invested capital. But this year Grace's final net will rebound as the result of the sale of Miller and other divestitures—capital transactions that obviously inflate the earnings picture.

Without these "extraordinary items," Grace's operating profits have not been glamorous, but neither have they been sickly. From 1960 to 1966 they climbed from $16 million to over $60 million, dipped in 1967, and recovered again last year to $58 million. On this basis Grace earnings on net worth worked out to about 10 percent, below those of Du Pont or Dow, to name two chemical companies, but above those of Union Carbide or Koppers or Pennwalt. In terms of earnings per share, however, which Peter Grace counts as the acid test of good management, the company has unquestionably lost forward momentum. Between 1960 and 1966 these swept up from $1.48 to $3.31, or an annual average of 14 percent compounded—a performance bound to attract any investor glancing at Grace. Yet last year earnings per share, on this basis, were down to $2.86, and in the first half of 1969 they skidded to $1.08, a drop of 35 percent from the same period in 1968. Earnings may brighten toward the end of this year when the Grace Line may be off the books, but obviously Peter Grace has quite a distance to go to restore steerage way and achieve what all good sailors want—sea room.

A Lurch to the Left

In attempting to do so Peter Grace has by no means written off Latin America, where W. R. Grace started operations over a century ago, and where it still has an investment of $130 million. Half of this investment is in Peru and the rest is scattered across other countries, notably Brazil, Colombia, and Mexico. In all these countries Grace is still doing well in chemicals, foods, and other ventures, and even in Peru its situation is not entirely hopeless. When the military junta expropriated Grace's sugar lands and sugar mills at Paramonga and Cartavio early last summer, they dealt more of a blow to Grace's pride than to its pocketbook. Over the years the company has lavished on Paramonga a vast amount of technical skill, which has made the plain between the Andes and the cold Pacific flower. Since its earliest days Grace has made itself part of the Peruvian economy and of the thrust of United States companies to better working and social conditions. At the stamp of a few pieces of legal paper by bemedaled generals, much of this effort went down the drain.

But if expropriation goes no further Grace's position is tenable, for the properties so far seized have a book value of only $25 million. Much more important to Grace are paper mills, which use bagasse from sugar cane as raw material, and chemical facilities, which produce caustic soda for papermaking and chlorine for making polyvinyl chloride. In August the generals threatened those facilities, too, and then in twenty-four hours rescinded the order. If that decision sticks, then Grace can make out, though the recent events have done nothing to increase confidence in military rule. What worries Grace is that the political winds across the South American continent have shifted. In the past the Army has been a symbol of stability, not perhaps the best form of stability, but stability for all that. But now the military in Peru have apparently lurched off to the left, discouraging that very inflow of capital which all Latin America so badly needs. The future of Latin America could be bright, says Peter Grace, if entrepreneurs, local and foreign, were given time. "The question," he adds, "is whether anybody is going to be given time."

For the moment, anyway, Latin America is for Grace at best a holding action. The crucial battle for profits is being fought out in the United States as well as Europe, where Grace, beginning in the fifties, diversified heavily into chemicals as a means of growth and expansion. But chemicals have proved to be an unpredictable genie and Grace has learned the hard way that the road to profits nowadays lies in specialization rather than in commodity chemicals like fertilizers, where competition is fierce and worldwide. Counting equity and long-term debt, Grace now has some $340 million of capital employed in fertilizers and other agricultural products (feed supplements, pesticides, herbicides, etc.). But in 1968 it earned a bare 3.4 percent after taxes on this enormous commitment as against an 11 percent return on capital employed in specialty chemicals that are sold largely to industry.

The poor showing in agricultural chemicals is all the more disappointing because Grace is no parvenu in this field. In the early days of the company it exploited the guano found on the rocks off the Peruvian coast, then invested heavily in Chilean nitrates, which it peddled to farmers in the United States; subsequently, Grace thought it could cash in on the wonders of nitrogen fixation and the growing United States farm demand for fertilizers of all kinds. In the mid-fifties Grace erected a big ammonia plant at Memphis, Tennessee, then turned to Trinidad, which has a plentiful supply of natural gas, a vital feedstock for ammonia production, and also commands access to United States ports and to Europe. In addition it established a position in phosphates through its acquisition of the Davison Chemical Co., which owned large phosphorous rock deposits in Florida.

What Grace didn't figure on was that the oil companies were also on the prowl for new outlets for their huge cracking facilities, and that between 1964 and 1968 new investment in fertilizers would run to some $4 billion, which, as Peter Grace points out, is more than the capital invested in the United States commercial airlines. The resulting collapse of prices has played ducks and drakes with part of Peter Grace's investment philosophy.

In betting on fertilizers, which require enormous fixed plants, he saw a way to leverage Grace's earnings per share through heavy borrowing. In 1959 Grace's long-term debt stood at about $164 million, or well under its shareholders' equity of $233 million. By 1967 debt had risen to over $500 million, or about equal to shareholders' equity. This increased debt, which went largely into financing agricultural chemical plants, has a relatively low rate of interest of around 5 percent, which amounts to only 2½ percent after taxes. This is fine if the total capital employed is yielding, say, 7 percent as it was in the mid-sixties. It is the devil when the yield has fallen even below the level of 1968 to a bare 2 percent this year. "The whole thing," reflects Peter Grace, "has been unbelievable."

The Other Side of the Lamp

But Grace has also abundantly proved that there are handsome profits to be made if you rub the Aladdin's lamp of modern chemistry the right way, and in the nonagricultural chemical field one success has led on to another in gratifying sequence. In 1968 sales of nonagricultural and mostly specialty chemical products ran to $615 million, and Grace's profit of 11 percent on capital employed bettered the over-all earnings on capital of Monsanto. As a welcome dividend from its acquisition of Davison Chemical in 1954, Grace makes those white grains of silica gel that go into filters for cigarette holders and, more important, is one of the biggest producers in the United States of catalysts for the oil and gas industry—those magical agents that have revolutionized the whole complex and steaming business of petroleum cracking. Its other early and key acquisition, the Dewey & Almy Chemical Co. of Cambridge, Massachusetts, has turned into a cornucopia of organic chemicals including sealants for the canning industry, additives used in paints and adhesives, and Cryovac shrink film used for packaging meats and other groceries.

In almost every case Grace protects its position by adding in a twist of special effort. Making sealants for cans doesn't sound hard until one reflects on the consequences of a defect in the product or its application. Grace designs the machinery used by the canning companies. In developing Cryovac film it has nursed the turkey business along from a sideline for a few farmers, who produced for the Thanksgiving and Christmas trade, into an industry that now grosses over $400 million annually. A modern automobile battery is only as good as the wafer-thin separators between its lead plates that keep the battery from shorting. Grace makes these, too, by impregnating special paper with phenol formaldehyde, and is developing a new plastic separator called Daramic, which it hopes to sell to G.M.'s Delco.

Prying further into the nooks and crannies of the chemical industry, Grace greatly strengthened its position by acquiring two other specialty companies. One is the DuBois Chemical Co. of Cincinnati, picked up in 1964 after a hot proxy fight. DuBois makes detergents and cleansers for hotels, hospitals, and restaurants, as well as for such industrial uses as scouring jet engines. This year it will earn over $5 million on $66 million of sales.

DuBois salesmen peddle the products of another Grace acquisition, the Dearborn Chemical Co., which makes chemicals that prevent scaling in industrial boilers and corrosion in water-cooling systems. It is also experimenting in the treatment of sewage and industrial wastes—a significant potential market in view of the federal government's antipollution campaign. The trouble is not just in finding the chemicals that will neutralize the wastes that have turned such bodies of water as Lake Erie into a kind of dead sea. It is also in persuading corporations, municipalities, and states to make the big initial investment in the filtering and other facilities that have to be in place before antipollution chemicals can go to work—facilities that often run into millions of dollars. Dearborn goes on the theory that half the battle of pollution is accurately defining the problem in the first place through running meticulous tests, and is betting that this kind of service will pay off in the years ahead. Dearborn had sales last year of only $13 million, but profits, calculated on 1969 returns, have risen at an average annual rate of 14 percent compounded—the kind of earning trend that Grace is looking for.

More dramatic has been the rise and proliferation of a cluster of enterprises stemming from Grace's acquisition in 1959 of the Hatco Chemical Co. for a bare $6 million. At the time Hatco didn't look like much, with an old-fashioned plant located on the Jersey flats, from whose steamy caldrons came phthalate plasticizers, stuff used for making various chemical plastics pliable and malleable. Its technical director, however, was a smart German-born chemist by the name of Alex Kaufman, whom Peter Grace spotted as a comer and to whom he has delegated wide responsibility. He has not regretted the choice. As late as 1963 the Hatco division had sales of $15 million with pretax profits of $1 million. This year Hatco is aiming toward sales of $195 million with pretax profits of $20 million.

This development has been accomplished by cleverly exploiting opportunities and, in Kaufman's phrase, using a "chemical building block" to get into a lot of higher margined products closer to the consumer. Originally, Hatco sold its plasticizers to the chemical industry for making polyvinyl film and sheeting such as goes into shower curtains, window shades, and upholstery. Now it makes these polyvinyls itself and also makes a wide range of polyesters that are used in fiber-glass boat hulls, various automotive parts such as small gears, and in the manufacture of artificial wood for the furniture trade. In developing these products Hatco became familiar with styling problems and has branched out into the styling of textiles, both natural and synthetic, through acquisition of the Golding Co., an old and lucrative textile converter. "We don't own textile mills," Kaufman points out, "but we are in textiles at the point where there are special profits to be made."

From styling plastics and textiles it was only a step in Kaufman's mind to styling other things—notably clothes—and early this year Hatco bought out John Meyer of Norwich (Connecticut). Meyer has made a name for itself in the higher priced women's clothing field. In Kaufman's view, these acquisitions are logical developments of his basic idea of always moving away from commodities, whether they be chemicals or textiles, toward some kind of specialization. No doubt there is considerable rationalization in this kind of thinking and the more skeptical might say that Kaufman moves wherever Kaufman and Peter Grace sniff profit. Be that as it may, he has so far succeeded, and in the next four years hopes to build total Hatco business to the $500-million mark.

The trouble, of course, is that it isn't every day that you pick up a winner like Hatco, and even the Hatco prognosis indicates that profits may be gained by leaping out of the chemical compound. "Chemicals gave us ten years of dynamic growth," reflected Peter Grace recently, but he concedes that it is more and more difficult to find openings, even in the industrial chemical field, where competition won't whittle away profit margins. For this reason he counts it fortunate that Grace in the early sixties began to put increasing emphasis on food products, and more recently has begun to explore the less tangible realm of what are loosely called service businesses.

Grace sidled into food via Europe when it acquired the Van Houten Co. of Holland, makers of one of the best chocolates—at least to adult tastes—on the market. It paid $8 million for the acquisition and ran into nothing but trouble. Van Houten wouldn't manage itself and Grace, as the years went by, found it couldn't manage Van Houten. The trouble was partly that Van Houten's European managers simply would not cater to mass tastes and had no desire to pretty up or sweeten up their product. A further trouble was that its plants needed renovation, facing Grace with the choice of putting up more cash or withdrawal. In 1969 it sold out 51 percent of its interest to Peter Paul, Inc., the candy company, but kept a 49-percent equity that entails little or no responsibility—a compromise that breaks Grace's normal rule of keeping its money only in companies that it can control.

But Van Houten at least whetted Grace's appetite for more food acquisitions, and it has made a lot of them. In Europe it owns that de Zaan Co., maker of cocoa and cocoa butter, and the Raak soft drink and bottling company, both in Holland; ice cream plants in Ireland, Denmark, and now in Italy, plus a chain of restaurants in France. In the United States it owns Ambrosia Chocolate Co., Leaf Brands (chewing gum and hard candies), Nalley's Fine Food (snacks and chili con carne), and SeaPak (frozen shrimp). When in 1966 Grace bought that 53-percent interest in Miller Brewing Co., maker of High Life, the so-called "champagne" of beers, it looked as if Grace was rounding out a new and profitable area of operations. Miller was a fine old-line company, which, if not as big as Pabst or Schlitz, had big possibilities for growth. At the time Peter Grace was already on the Miller board, knew its operations thoroughly, and was on good terms with both Mrs. Lorraine John Mulberger and her brother, Harry John, of Milwaukee, who had inherited control of the company from its founder.

By dint of considerable persuasion, plus $36 million, Grace finally jarred loose Mrs. Mulberger's 53-percent majority interest, and then went on to deal with her brother. Here, however, the company ran into a stone wall. A deeply religious man, Harry John had put all but one phase of his inheritance into a charitable trust, and he saw no reason for changing this arrangement. Inevitably there developed a split in working philosophy. Grace was all for expanding Miller; Harry John was for paying out substantial dividends for the benefit of various philanthropies. Meanwhile, brewing shares were advancing briskly in the stock market, and by last year Peter Grace concluded that if he could not run Miller the way he wanted to run it, then maybe it was time to pull out if he could get the right price. As matters turned out, pulling out proved even more arduous than getting in.

As a starter Peter Grace approached Donald Kendall, president of PepsiCo, making it clear that if Grace sold, it wanted cash or pretty close to cash equivalent. Kendall was definitely interested at a price of $120 million, but he himself lost precious time in trying to buy out Harry John's holdings. When that failed he and Grace last spring signed an agreement in principle—subject, however, to negotiation of a definitive contract. What happened thereafter is clouded in hot dispute, but on Grace's account PepsiCo shifted its terms from $20 million in cash, plus a note redeemable in September 1969, to much less advantageous maturities—a change that had to go back to Grace's board of directors. Meanwhile, in late May, Peter Grace, impatient with such dickerings, spied another prospect in Philip Morris, which had increased its tender offer for the acquisition of Canadian Breweries Ltd.—an offer that fell through. In less than two weeks Peter Grace and Joseph Cullman, chairman of Philip Morris, had worked out and concluded an all-cash deal of $130 million, leaving PepsiCo in the cold. PepsiCo has brought a suit, charging conspiracy and breach of contract, which seeks to have the Miller shares returned to W. R. Grace so that it could sell them to PepsiCo. Grace points out there never was a contract, but even in the event that the courts should hold with PepsiCo, Grace would presumably receive $120 million, and still profit handsomely from its Miller involvement.

A Third Concept

The real question facing Peter Grace in terms of the longer future is where he is going to find alternative investments as good as Miller in the food business or elsewhere, and what he is going to do with additional liquidity flowing in from the impending sale of the Grace Line for $44 million to Spyros P. Skouras. To be sure, liquid funds now earn handsome returns in the money market but they could also be a temptation for a raid on Grace itself by some other prowling conglomerate—especially since Peter Grace and his immediate family control less than 2 percent of the stock. Peter Grace discounts this possibility sharply, pointing out that many of his shareholders stem from old family companies like Dewey & Almy that would think twice before accepting any kind of cash-tender offer that would involve brutal capital-gains taxes. The more pressing consideration is that if Grace is to resume its course as a growth company it must put its cash into tangible earning properties.

In facing up to this challenge Peter Grace points out that thus far he has followed two "concepts"—chemicals and foods. What attracts him is a third concept—namely "services." In this century, he notes, the whole aspect of the United States economy has changed from one where manufacturing held the key and rising position to one where services employ over 50 percent of the labor force. To be sure, services as defined by the economists include a very mixed bag of tricks—electric-power generation and telephone services, for instance, in which Grace is not interested, plus at least two fields from which it has withdrawn or is withdrawing, banking and shipping. When Peter Grace uses the term it is in a narrower sense.

In Europe production of foods has led to running restaurants. In the United States the success of Hatco shows that it is possible to edge out from fuming chemical plants into styling both chemical products and textiles. In 1968 Grace bought a company called Devcoa, which surveys and assembles real-estate sites and builds facilities for various clients, including oil companies needing new gasoline service stations and retail stores. More recently Grace has organized a "new enterprises" group to provide venture capital to small companies and budding entrepreneurs. It is backing, for instance, an outfit that manufactures a sportsman's vehicle that will operate on land and on water—a first step, perhaps, to entering the recreation-leisure field. It has also invested in the fast-growing education area through Applied Decision Systems Inc., a company formed by some bright young Harvard men. Finally and importantly, Grace is edging over into electronics through a company specializing in inventory control systems for retail stores, and through Multicomp Inc. of Waltham, Massachusetts, which is in computer time sharing and programming.

These are pretty small ventures but they point in new directions, and they could eventually absorb a lot of capital. In exploring them, Peter Grace has become aware that he may have to change Grace's way of doing business. In the case of early acquisitions like Davison and Dewey & Almy, Grace purchased complete control. In forming new ventures today he finds that he can only get entrepreneurial talent by giving that talent an equity in the new company. Indeed, he sometimes wonders whether he can keep Grace's present managerial team together without some form of reorganization. Most of the team undoubtedly hold Grace shares options, but the earnings from the groups they run are highly uneven. One idea would be to set up some of these groups as separate corporate entities that would be controlled by Grace but would sell stock in the public market. Grace managers could then be given stock options in these profitable enterprises.

Still another idea that Peter Grace has toyed with is to spin off the corporation's big investment in fertilizers and agricultural products entirely, and thus relieve Grace of the big and obvious drag on its present earnings. There are, however, some compelling reasons against this radical move. Grace has spent millions building up its agricultural distribution system—one of the best in the business. Fertilizer prices may come back, with a sharp leverage on profits. Finally, it is through its agricultural investment that Grace holds not only rich mineral deposits in Florida but also very considerable land areas which can be developed. And in an uncertain world Peter Grace believes that land may be the prize investment of all. Indeed, he says, "I wish we had more of it."

So for the present, anyway, Peter Grace is apt to stick with what he has got, and what he has got, counting the bright record of industrial chemicals, is not so bad. "It would have been nice," he ruminated recently, "if we had foreseen the boom in office equipment, and could have picked up a company like Burroughs." But that is easier to see now than at the time, and Peter Grace is not one to lament too much over lost opportunities. In one way or another he is determined to lift Grace earnings from 10 percent on equity to 15 percent. "That is a minimal target." And certainly he now has the cash on hand to explore new terrain. What will count in the years ahead is how Grace deploys that cash and, to borrow a phrase from Keynes, its "impregnable liquidity." It's not exactly an easy task but—come to think of it—there are probably a good many corporate executives these days who wish they had a similar problem.

PART II

Bumps and Forebodings

The Perils of the
Multi-Market Corporation

LAMMOT DU PONT COPELAND, president of Du Pont, was asked not long ago why his company wasn't going conglomerate or diversifying into new lines, as so many other corporations in the United States were doing. "Running a conglomerate," Copeland replied dryly, "is a job for management geniuses, not for ordinary mortals like us at Du Pont." Copeland's crack went straight to the heart of what some think could turn out to be the next great management problem in this country. Now that the long economic expansion of the 1960s is finally tapering off, the conglomerates—better described as multi-industry or multi-market companies—may be moving into a period that separates ordinary mortals from management geniuses.

Multi-market companies are probably the most portentous business phenomenon of the postwar era. For nearly twenty years they have been hurdling traditional industry boundaries and moving into different and quite unrelated markets. They have been doing so, it appears, chiefly by acquisition and merger, as distinguished from internal development. It used to be that the bulk of mergers were either "horizontal" (into identical or complementary products) or "vertical" (into the products of suppliers and customers). But according to Federal Trade Commission

77

figures, no less than 70 percent of all important mergers and acquisitions between 1960 and 1965 were conglomerate or multi-market, and only 13 percent were horizontal.

The conglomerates that have got the most attention, appropriately enough, are the ones that were deliberately created or built up that way. The three that have set the style are Litton, Textron, and FMC, and they have become almost classic examples of "pure" multi-market companies. But such comparative newcomers to the industrial world, although archetypical of the movement, are actually outnumbered by "old" corporations that for one reason or another have decided to till other fields than the ones they made their names in. Among these are Peter Grace's W. R. Grace & Co., formerly a steamship operator and South American trader, which diversified into such activities as chemicals and foods; Harold Geneen's International Telephone & Telegraph, which has added to its fold a wide variety of products from textbooks to Avis rental cars; the Sarnoffs' R.C.A., which has bought Random House and, not to be outdone by I.T.T., offered $185 million for Hertz; and Donald Kircher's Singer Co., which used the money it made in sewing machines to buy into indoor climate-control and textile machinery and office equipment.

The multi-market corporation manifestly derives a certain strength from its disparate union; even if things go bad in one division, the company's total performance may hold up very well, and the resources of the combination can be marshaled to cure division ailments. But the headquarters managements of such companies also have one immense problem in common; theirs is a vastly harder and more complex job than managing a homogeneous or single-market company. Top multi-market management is responsible for the whole firm; it justifies its existence only if the divisions perform better or more efficiently as divisions than they could as independent companies. But a multi-market company is also by definition a multi-adversity company. As the trials and tribulations of corporate history testify abundantly, a single-market company, even in good times, runs into troubles that can strain if not floor the most gifted managers. Because a corporation composed of a lot of different divisions can encounter more adversities than the more homogeneous company, it may need more top-level management talent to deal with them.

Recently a large multi-market corporation discovered almost too late that one of its divisions whose current return was excellent was failing to keep its potential up to that of its competitors. Fortunately, times were good and headquarters boasted enough talent to cope with the problem. Had misfortune afflicted several divisions at once, however, that corporation might have found itself in a bad way. The basic dilemma of the multi-market company thus becomes plain: if it stocks up with enough talent to deal simultaneously with many adversities, including recession, it could find itself with an unwieldly headquarters staff that could impose an almost intolerable burden on the divisions. But if the headquarters talent inventory is too lean, it could find itself falling behind its competitors.

A Way of Avoiding Extinction

Despite such evident hazards, there have been some compelling reasons why so many corporations have decided to "go multi" in recent years. A good many of the forces behind the trend are the same ones that have long impelled corporations to expand—forces in which personal opportunism and economic opportunities are inextricably mingled. Ambitious men, as they always have, crave to build durable empires, and the bright ones know where the opportunities lie. Most of the "new" multi-management corporations, including Litton, Textron, and FMC, were founded by ambitious men who were resolved to expand even before they knew what their expansion rationale or strategy would be. But they formulated their strategy astutely, taking advantage of technological advances and swiftly changing markets.

The corporation, like the individual, has a tropism for living and growing, but unlike the individual it need not die. Some older, established, single-product companies diversify in order to avoid obsolescence or even extinction. By spreading their assets over many different products, they try to reduce their aggregate risk. They also diversify to offset seasonal and cyclical fluctuations in existing markets, to get into lines with bigger potential rewards, and to make better use of their capital resources, particularly when they generate more cash than they can use in the business. Some corporations, aiming to save years of time and a lot of money, buy a company for its well-developed product or its management or both, so they can enter markets not as new but as established competitors.

Opportunities have been very plentiful. More and more tightly held or family-owned companies are for sale because their owners need or want liquidity, and they usually can get more of it by selling out than by going public and putting their own stock on the market. A number of small companies founded on new technologies haven't the resources to develop their potential, and many lagging older ones haven't the money to take the risks they need to take to realize theirs; both find it easy and profitable to sell out to stronger companies.

The powerful expansion-minded corporation, in turn, can make irresistibly good deals. If it decides to pay cash for a company whose stock is selling at ten times earnings, it can well afford to borrow money at 6 percent or more to pay the bill. In so doing it buys $1 worth of annual earnings for $10, and it pays only 60 cents interest a year, or less than 30 cents after taxes, for that $1 in earnings. If the buyer's own stock is selling at a high price-earnings ratio, sellers whose stock commands a lower price-earnings ratio will stand in line for a stock deal, hoping to trade or sell their shares above market price.

One especially powerful reason for the popularity of the conglomerate merger has been the recent aggressiveness of Antitrust. This has made companies reluctant to enter fields closely related to their own, where merger might actually have made the most business sense. Although the forces of Antitrust are gathering mountains of evidence for an assault on the multi-market movement, they have not yet proved that conglomerates on balance weaken competition as much as they strengthen it. So expansion-minded companies with money or access to money have been unwilling or unable to use it in horizontal or vertical expansion and naturally have been drawn to new fields.

Years ago they might have hesitated. But with the development of new techniques like scientific decision making —and particularly "exception" reporting, the profit-center concept, and computerized information systems—managers are much more confident that they can handle an aggregation of different companies than they were, say, twenty years ago. Most multi-expansionists do not go so far as to say they should or can take over any kind of business, no matter how "different." Although their acquisitions have illustrated just about every possible degree of relationship to one another, they prefer them to have some "mutuality of interest" or "concentricity," both of which designate some kind of meaningful relationship. Another of their favorite words is "synergy," sometimes described as the two-plus-two-equals-five effect, or the combination of two things whose joint effect is greater than the sum of the parts. To illustrate, when a company proposes to buy another very different company, it tries to pick one that will add something of value to its capabilities, such as an exceptional sales or research department. Sometimes the synergy is so intangible that it serves more as an excuse than a reason for expanding. "You get them interested," says one seller about buyers he has met, "and they find the synergy." Even the most ambitious empire builder yearns to justify his ambition with economics.

A voluble and enthusiastic body of thought has dubbed the strategically planned multi-market firm the "free-form company," and hailed it as one of the greatest economic happenings of our time, the flowering of the postwar trend toward the professionalization of American management. The new management techniques, the argument goes, have generated a new breed of young, ambitious, creative free-form managers, possessing an uncommon degree of generalized—as distinguished from specialized—management talent. Adaptable and versatile, with minds spacious enough to see beyond the company and yet disciplined and informed enough to solve its special problems, these managers have an uncanny eye for growth situations, especially those in new technologies. They are impatient with protocol and scorn memo writing; they use jet planes like taxis and are perennially on the move, inspecting plants the world over, soaking up wisdom here and discharging it there. They handle several businesses at once, and handle them more effectively, not to say more brilliantly, than the old-time specialists handled a single business. Some enthusiasts see the free-form company with its free-form managers as the prototype of all sizable firms a generation hence.

What makes this all so plausible is that some multi-market corporations have so far shown a high capacity for increasing their earnings. Litton, Textron, and FMC, all companies with seemingly unrelated lines of products, are three of the fastest-growing billion-dollar United States corporations. Over the past six years Litton's sales have quintupled, and those of Textron and FMC have tripled. And their profits have at least kept pace with sales.

By far the most important step in making a multi-market corporation work is to get into the right things in the first place. Nobody can yet say that the leading companies have made all the right moves. But they seem to have shown great skill in expanding not only internally but by acquisition, a process whose parlous intricacies have been the subject of whole books. For the most part, they have tried not to pay "too much" for their acquisitions and have avoided going excessively into debt. Occasionally they have picked up companies selling at less than book value. But they took care to avoid buying companies merely because they were cheap, and they bought cheap ones only when pretty sure of their unrealized potentialities.

Most have made a policy of seeking out well-managed companies. "Buying an outfit that has to be restaffed is anathema to Textron," says Chairman Rupert Thompson. "We buy a profit center and expect it to do a terrific job— with our coordination." But some corporations will buy a "bargain" if they are sure of its unrealized profitability. "We prefer a company with good management because we're growing so fast we're thin in people who can step into important jobs," says James Hait, chairman of FMC. "But we may take a company with a good product where top management is ready to step down." A good example was American Viscose, which FMC bought in 1964 for $114 million cash. The financial world had some doubts about Avisco, but basically it was a great opportunity, and after a few changes it sprang to highly profitable life as an FMC division.

There are dozens of complex techniques for financing acquisitions, but the main choice falls between purchasing with stock or cash and exchanging stock in a so-called pooling-of-interest arrangement. Paying in cash has the advantage of not diluting equity; paying in either stock or cash has the advantage of making the payment the basis for tax-deductible depreciation. By way of extreme example, if a company shells out $60 million in cash for an enterprise that carries depreciated assets of $10 million, it may be able to write up those assets to an appraised value of, say, $30 million. Thus the buyer greatly increases tax-deductible depreciation. Although earnings thenceforth may suffer for a time, the tax saving increases cash flow, and so puts the company in a better over-all financial position. Whether it pays in stock or cash, however, the purchasing company is obliged to enter as good will in its books the difference between the price it pays and the appraised value of the acquired company's assets.

But in the pooling-of-interest arrangement, which simply lumps the assets of the two companies together, the buyer does not write up depreciable assets, and so he can maximize profits, at least for a considerable time. This arrangement has stood Litton in good stead. Once Litton got a reputation for acumen and growth, its stock gained and maintained a high price-earnings ratio. Chairman Charles Thornton and President Roy Ash kept it that way by picking prospects with good profits and a lower price-earnings ratio than Litton's own. Some of the company's most important deals have been purchases for cash. Consequently, most acquisitions have added more to Litton's earnings per share than to the number of its shares outstanding. "Roy has a chain-letter operation going for him," says one admiring competitor. Ash's rejoinder: "You'd never know it by our work hours."

Besides expanding sagaciously, the leading multi-market companies, so far, seem to be skillfully operated. Essentially, each has relied on a rather small headquarters staff to run many different divisions, usually organized into groups of common or related products. Headquarters consists of corporate legal, financial, and public-relations departments. These departments, working with group vice presidents or coordinators, control the divisions. Headquarters usually maintains a staff of management experts to help the divisions "when necessary." Thus, the theory goes, the divisions are provided with both the money and the expertise they would not have had by themselves. But the divisions are allowed and even encouraged to exercise a high degree of autonomy, with ample "motivation" in the form of generous bonuses and profit-sharing schemes based on performance.

The prophets of the free-form corporation define it as basically scientific, professional, and entrepreneurial, with a commitment to something larger than the mere humdrum operation of a business. They also distinguish it from what they call the General Motors School, which in the words of one market letter "views the corporate manager as a specialized taskmaster with defined responsibilities within a tightly structured system of communications and decision making." This letter even alludes to the "obsolete world of Alfred P. Sloan," the man who first dealt with the paradox of decentralization in a big way by showing how a certain amount of decentralization can be used to strengthen headquarters control. What G.M.'s management was to the past, the letter implies, free-form management is to the future.

This seems to be going too far. Efficiency and entrepreneurship are not mutually exclusive; one cannot flourish without the other. Only a small percentage of managers can be daring entrepreneurs, just as only a tiny percentage of the human race can be financiers or corporation executives. In a free economy, efficiency and productivity must in the very nature of things be the overwhelming preoccupation of management as a whole. The vast bulk of management talent is devoted to producing and distributing goods and services; and the nation's living standards continue to rise only if the productivity of the output of goods and services rises—i.e., if their cost in man-hours declines. The social test of managerial effectiveness, over the long run, is how well the nation's resources are used.

The Immemorial Function of the Market

Innovation is a major source of rising productivity. But even in a world of radical change, innovation must occur at a pace that encourages production to increase faster than man-hours; and the job of regulating that pace is the immemorial function of the market. The producer who too often changes his product or substitutes expensive new ones prices himself out of the market. But the producer who knows how to use change and innovation to provide more for the money expands his market. In other words, creativity and risk taking, in a free democratic economy, must exist primarily to serve productivity.

Only a prudent as well as a venturesome manager can combine efficiency and productivity. And only a prudent manager can cope with the competitive and cyclical adversities that every mature firm encounters almost without respite, and to which every new creative firm is sooner or later heir. But no manager can be prudent unless he knows as much about his business as he possibly can. It is true that techniques such as the profit-center concept and "exception" reporting are constantly enlarging the puissance of the bright manager. But the question is whether there is really a substitute, even at top levels, for the manager with years of specialized experience.

One man who thinks not is Joel Dean, professor of business economics at Columbia and head of Joel Dean Associates, economic consultants. In collaboration with Winfield Smith of the University of Chicago, Dean recently contributed a chapter on profitability and company size to a book entitled *The Corporate Merger*. "The belief that managerial ability is general and transferable appeals not only to journalists, novelists, politicians, and the general public, but to successful managers as well," Dean and Smith wrote. "We believe the weight of evidence is to the contrary, that managerial ability is generally tied quite closely to the particular industry setting in which it develops and operates. A good manager's intuitions, like those of a good card player, come from his long experience with the special rules, technology, and markets of a particular industry; only in extraordinary individuals—so few as to be practically negligible—do we find the ability to absorb a new game intellectually and then compete successfully with experienced players. The case is different when there are no experienced players, as is true of new industries, or perhaps the Department of Defense. When practical men go out to find a manager, their behavior is as we would predict. Executive Search specialists discourage industry jumping, and successful executives change industries much less often than they change firms."

Some students of management take issue with Dean. They point out that financial, research, and legal expertise transcend industry boundaries, and that outsiders such as management advisers often bring insights to problems that stump the information-crammed specialists. J. Fred Weston, professor of business economics and finance at U.C.L.A., goes further. Although the skills of technical or division vice presidents are pretty much geared to their industrial experience, he says, the skills of the top managers who direct them are "transferable." But Dean replies that the top manager must know a lot about his business in order to direct his division heads effectively; his productivity, in others words, depends on his knowledge. Although Dean concedes that new techniques allow the top manager to take on more responsibilities than he used to, he also insists that the overall management job can still grow too large—i.e., the cost of controlling and coordinating the corporation can rise faster than the benefits the corporation gets from that control.

Dean accordingly advises his diversification-minded clients to think of growth not as an independent goal but primarily as a way of achieving optimum size, and to judge a proposed diversification or merger exactly as they would another capital investment—i.e., on the basis of its rate of return. If they have accumulated more cash than they can profitably invest in their own businesses and don't want to pay it out as dividends because most of the dividends will be taxed away, let them buy up their stock and other securities on the market. In effect the companies thus pass the money on to their stockholders as a capital gain, and so allow the market to allocate capital.

The corporate practice of internal financing has for years been bypassing and drying up the capital market, which, in theory at least, is as well worth preserving as any other market. An important economic disadvantage of the multi-market company is that it not only bypasses the capital market but may present a misleading picture to stockholders. Thanks to Mother Hubbard profit-and-loss statements that can hide both the superlative performance of some divisions and the dismal performance of others, financial analysts have little way of telling how a multi-market corporation is really doing. That is one reason some people believe that multi-market companies should report sales and profits by divisions.

Where Diversification Failed

But the great job ahead of multi-market companies, particularly those that have sprung up in the past fifteen years, is to cope with the problems of maturity. Like all United States corporations, they have been favored by good times— times in which steadily rising demand has enabled many second-rate and even marginal companies to turn in good performances. But competition inevitably increases, either because competitors become more proficient or because demand temporarily tapers off, or both. The going inevitably becomes harder, and many an acquisition that looked like a sure moneymaker runs into unforeseen trouble. If the multi-market corporation hasn't enough knowledgeable management at the top, it can run into trouble too.

The history of United States corporate diversification certainly is not lacking in examples of trouble. How many or what percentage of diversifications have been downright failures nobody can say simply because the real record is usually concealed in all-embracing annual reports. But enough details get in the news to suggest that the conglomerate way of life has been at least as rough in practice as it is in theory. Back in 1956, after Olin Mathieson moved into many new markets in an offensive of acquisitions, the company's executives predicted sales of $1.2 billion and net of $111 million by 1960; today, after five years of heroic "restructuring," the company has still not reached that goal. Starting in 1957, cigarette maker Philip Morris tried to diversify into packing papers, toiletries, razor blades, and chewing gum; nine years later only chewing gum was a real success. Blaw-Knox, the steel-mill equipment manufacturer, was making $4.16 a share in 1956, when it diversified into road-building and food-processing equipment and construction contracts for chemical and petroleum plants. By 1965, profits had slid to $1.61 a share.

Not long ago Stanley Miller, former professor at the Harvard Business School, took three years to study the postwar history of a dozen diversification-minded auto-industry suppliers including Arundel Metal Corp., Briggs, Budd, Hupp, and Motor Products. The result, a book entitled *The Management Problems of Diversification* (John Wiley, 1963), draws some arresting conclusions about the difficulties in making diversification work. The basic creed of multi-market companies, as we have seen, is to let the divisions alone as much as possible. In practice, Miller found, this was not so easy as it sounds. Once an acquisition was made, corporate headquarters usually got more and more involved; it could not, for all its resolutions about division autonomy, leave things to the former managers no matter how competent. Arundel, for example, started to diversify in 1953 with well-defined goals. After years of painful searching, it got into plastics, electronic equipment, and controls by acquiring three companies. But Arundel's top management found its troubles were just beginning. The acquired companies now had access to new capital, but this meant new problems that cried for help; and headquarters had to get deeply involved or abdicate its responsibilities. Before participating in new-product decisions, for example, it had to become thoroughly familiar with a proposed product and its market.

Miller's research also casts doubt on other multi-market credos, including the one that it is possible to buy a company's management talent and keep it. In most cases the chief executives of the acquired companies had to be replaced by new division heads, even when headquarters wanted the old managers to stay on. The problem of management succession, of course, is one that only top management can solve, and the solution can take a lot of time.

"The greatest danger in diversification," Miller concludes, "is that it tends to separate management talents and interests from the every-day content of a particular business environment. A system of reports can help replace the intuition brought about by years of association with the people and practices of a particular industry. But when talent becomes too far separated from content, it becomes difficult to interpret in a meaningful way the figures in the reports. Although diversification offers a natural means of keeping pace with a changing world, we must not forget the old principle that the people who run a corporation should know as much as possible about the business they manage."

Nobody seems better aware of all this than some of the well-run multi-market companies themselves. For all their talk of division autonomy, most of them are not quite so decentralized as they sound, and they are growing less so. They are beefing up headquarters capabilities and tightening controls. For they are encountering the problem that has plagued every sizable organization from General Motors to the Soviet Union: How much local autonomy can you allow without losing control? How do you centralize control without getting bogged down in detail?

The more mature companies that have expanded into many markets have no illusions about the problem. "One of the major difficulties in managing a diversified business," says Felix Larkin, executive vice president of W. R. Grace, "is the amount of knowledge the central manager has to have. While we try to decentralize and localize responsibility, we can't have a loose federation of independent states." Singer has been through a ten-year diversification program, and is now a kind of multi-market company with only half its sales accounted for by sewing machines. President Donald Kircher hates to see headquarters grow too big, but finds it hard to dispense with its functions. "Some of the big conglomerates have outstanding management," he says, "but those that don't are bound to have serious problems. A recession would put them to the test. It would call for a great deal of management, and some companies don't have enough to deal with trouble in big doses."

To Manage Is to Know

FMC, too, has found it wise to maintain a much larger headquarters staff than some of the newer multi-market companies. The central corporate group numbers about 150, but this figure does not include a market-analysis group or an industrial-engineering department that assists divisions on latest production techniques. The corporation also maintains central research and development departments that explore new fields for the divisions. So without taking away any responsibility from the divisions, FMC monitors them closely, and is prepared to move in on a situation needing attention. "I'd be frightened," says President James Hait, "if we were in the shoes some people are in, those who acquire companies in totally unrelated fields. Unless you've got an organization with a lot of talent that can strengthen and sharpen your acquisitions, it looks dangerous."

Litton, as noted, is deeply committed to division autonomy because it feels specialized division managers can handle their affairs better and "recognize areas of opportunity" better than corporation headquarters. But Roy Ash deplores the phrase "free-form management" and likes to think of Litton's techniques as modern extensions of Alfred Sloan's principles, with tools that did not exist in Sloan's day. So Litton acts on the truism that management must manage, and that to manage, it must *know*. "The more decisions you delegate to others," says Ash, "the more important it is to know how others are making them."

One of the few multi-market companies that do not seem to be moving in the direction of more central control is Textron. Thompson insists that his technique consists mainly of selection, coordination, and ample incentives. There is some evidence that Thompson coordinates more than he says, that Textron talks about autonomy as much as it encourages real autonomy, and that it has mastered the fine art of planting ideas in a division manager's head and then agreeing with him when he comes up with them. But the big difference between Textron and the other multis is that Thompson runs it with something of the flexibility of an investment trust. He buys what seems best for his purposes, and if it doesn't pan out within a reasonable time in terms of his extremely high profit goal (25 percent on net invested capital before taxes), he gets rid of it. In 1963, for example, Thompson sold Amerotron (textiles), which was making "only" $5,500,-000 on sales of $72 million; last June he sold Weinbrenner (shoes), which was making "only" 15 percent on net invested capital.

But many multi-market companies seem to have committed themselves to planned expansion programs that take time for the divisions to work out. Even if they could acquire and discard at will, some are naturally too proud or stubborn to do so. So their big problem is relatively easy to define. In the fullness of time, as sundry adversities rear their ugly heads, multi-managers must justify themselves by developing effective control systems, and yet prevent the control function from growing to the point where it doesn't justify its size. Those who have not already done so will find themselves poring over the pages of Alfred Sloan, who was confronted nearly fifty years ago with essentially the same problem. The big difference is that, because G.M. products were closely related, Sloan's job was much easier.

The Merger Movement
Rides High

THE GREAT CONGLOMERATE movement is generating wide-spread doubt, apprehension, and even dismay. Aggressive empire builders, displaying the legendary boldness and imagination of the great American business barons, are falling over one another in their haste to create large multi-market companies. And in the process many are engaging in practices and confecting situations that someday may land their resplendently varied structures in deep trouble.

These latter-day empire builders are violating no laws and flouting no accounting conventions. But just as there are good and bad ways of running a company, so there are good and bad ways of putting conglomerates together. What many conglomerators are doing is not paying sufficient attention to the necessity for operating successfully in mundane profit-and-loss terms when the creative acquiring is over. Some of their sharpest critics, significantly, are "conservative" multi-market managers like President Roy Ash of Litton Industries and President G. William Miller of Textron, who have carefully formulated their notions of what a multi-market corporation should be and have stuck with them. Both have denounced "arithmetic mergers" and "mergers by numbers," or combinations in which sound planning for internal growth is subordinated to the mere piling up of assets. Miller describes the arithmetic-merger approach as "business fundamentals be damned, jazz up the stock and on to the races." More, he characterizes it as a great danger to the economy, and hopes that the SEC and the stock exchanges can refine their controls to deal with it.

Meantime the conglomerate tide has swollen into a colossal flood of mergers and take-overs. The tide seems virtually unstoppable; even a sharp stock-market decline, Wall Street believes, would probably stay it only for a while. An important force in the movement is the tender offer or take-over bid, in which the aggressor offers the target company's stockholders a price so irresistible that they tender him enough stock for control. Thus the stockholder, relegated by Adolf Berle and other noncontemporary economists to a limbo of impotent ownership, has found himself inadvertently practicing Stockholder Power. By one count there were 249 tender offers last year, and that number does not measure the full importance of the take-over boom. A great proportion of all mergers last year were consummated, often hastily and ill-advisedly, because a company wanted to keep from being taken over by an aggressor.

The targets of this aggression are some of the most upright, prudent, powerful, and self-assured corporations in the land. Self-assurance is fading. Proud old names have already been taken over, and dozens of verteran executives have been sacked. Foreboding, frustration, and even fear are epidemic in perhaps three out of five big corporate headquarters. Anguished executives who should be minding the shop are instead behaving as if they were up to some underhanded adventure, spending long hours counseling with lawyers, management consultants, proxy specialists, and public-relations men skilled in the art of forfending take-overs.

Conglomeration enthusiasts, including a swarm in Wall Street investment houses, are shedding few tears of sympathy, and taking every opportunity to discharge homilies on the mission of the conglomerate. The conglomerate, they argue, aids and abets efficiency and productivity by funneling capital to enterprises in which it can be used most profitably. It is ridding the economy of backward, stuffy management "that doesn't deserve to have control of all those

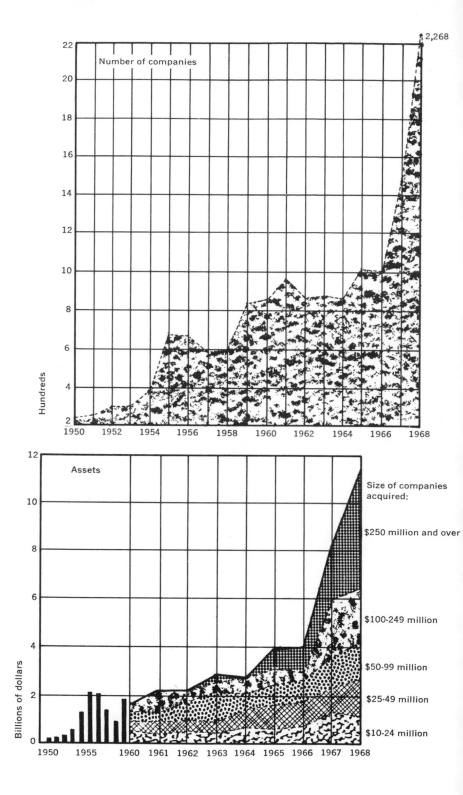

assets," and prodding lethargic management to do better. It is revitalizing complacent enterprises that have grown fat and sluggish in sheltered corners of the marketplace. It is giving the shareholder the power to overturn management. No doubt anticipating antitrust intervention, conglomerators also argue that conglomeration means a freer, more flexible, and on the whole a more competitive economy. And they're all sure they are in the main groove of economic history. Fred Sullivan, chairman of Walter Kidde & Co., recently told a group of bankers that going conglomerate is "the American way of business," and will soon be "obligatory" for all United States business. Nicholas Salgo, the Hungarian born ex-realtor who started Bangor Punta with a potato railroad and an expropriated Cuban sugar company, predicts that in ten years there will be only 200 major industrial companies in the United States, all conglomerate.

Mergers by Numbers

The fact remains, however, that the process of putting conglomerates together tends to expand stock prices long before it expands the economic values on which stock prices ultimately depend. Moreover, this tendency, thanks to the efforts of the latter-day empire builders, is becoming steadily more pronounced. In 1967 the average aggressor company paid 18 times earnings for the average target; last

---

The Biggest Merger Movement Ever
Both in Number and in Asset Value, Acquisitions Are Soaring

There have been merger movements in the United States before. One began in the 1890s and another in the 1920s; each lasted about a decade. But the current merger movement is lasting longer and is immensely bigger. In 1968 the number of mergers (chart above) was more than ten times larger than in 1950. The chart below, which shows the dollar value of the assets of acquired companies worth $10 million or more, also shows the trend toward bigger and bigger acquisitions. Figures for both charts, compiled by the Federal Trade Commission, include only mergers of manufacturing and mining companies, which in 1968 totaled 2,268. According to estimates by W. T. Grimm & Co. of Chicago, mergers of all kinds totaled 4,462 in 1968.

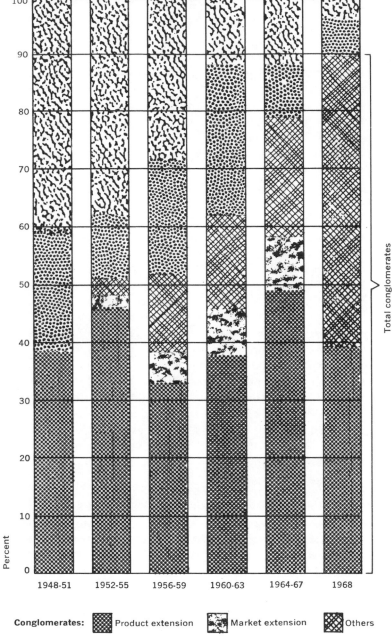

Percent

100 — 90 — 80 — 70 — 60 — 50 — 40 — 30 — 20 — 10 — 0

1948-51   1952-55   1956-59   1960-63   1964-67   1968

Total conglomerates

Conglomerates: Product extension   Market extension   Others

Non-conglomerates: Vertical   Horizontal

year the figure shot up to 25. On the face of it, this seems an excessively high price unless the acquisitions will boost real earnings of the conglomerates substantially. Sometimes, moreover, the acquiring company adds sweeteners that boost the price still further. It trades, say, $75 million worth of its stock for another company's stock, and guarantees stockholders that their shares will be worth $100 million in a year. If the shares haven't risen that much, the acquiring company issues enough new ones to bring payment up to $100 million.

One very important factor often making conglomeration a numbers game is that so many acquisitions involve stock-market prices. This can give the appearance of growth where some exists, and often produces a chain-letter effect whose terminal stages may be painful. And like a strange new virus, it can and does infect even the most conservative of multi-market companies. Generally the acquirer is a company whose stock is selling at a relatively high price-earnings ratio. Usually the p/e is high because the company has demonstrated a capacity to grow at an exceptional rate—although frequently an outfit skilled in public relations, by talking imaginatively about its plans and prospects, can command a much higher p/e ratio than actual performance warrants. But for whatever reason, the company is well

---

The Conglomerate Take-Over

Conglomerate mergers, in the minority twenty years ago, have come to account for a lopsided majority of all mergers in the United States. What's more, mergers in which the acquiring and acquired companies have nothing in common have come to dominate the increase in conglomerate unions. What the Federal Trade Commission calls product-extension conglomerate mergers, in which a company acquires another producing a related product, have dwindled in relative importance. And what the FTC calls market-extension mergers, in which a company acquires a similar but geographically separate company, have practically disappeared. The 1950 Celler-Kefauver Amendment to the Clayton Act increased the barriers to nonconglomerate mergers, both horizontal (in which a company takes over a competitor) and vertical (in which it takes over a supplier or distributor). The chart shows the pattern for mergers that involve manufacturing and mining companies.

thought of by investors and does command a relatively high price-earning ratio.

Any time such a company—for that matter any company —buys another whose shares are selling at a lower price-earnings ratio, earnings per share of the merged company in the first year of its existence will inevitably be higher than those of the acquiring company in the previous year. Contrariwise, any time a company buys another with a higher price-earnings ratio, the combination will turn up with lower earnings per share. This sounds incredible. It says that a conglomerator is better off—or *seems* better off— merging with an inferior organization than merging with a superior one. Yet it is so, and a little simple arithmetic demonstrates why.

Assume Company A has a million shares earning $1 each; they are selling at $30 a share because the market judges A's growth favorably. Now assume Company B also has a million shares earning $1 each; they are selling at only $10 a share because B shows no internal growth at all. So A generously offers B's stockholders $15 a share, either in cash, which it can easily raise, or preferably in A's own stock, which has the advantage of exempting B's stockholders from an immediate capital-gains tax. In other words, A trades 500,000 of its own shares for all of B's million shares. So the new company is capitalized at 1,500,-000 shares earning $2 million. This works out not to $1 a share, as before the merger, but to $1.33. Although nothing really has changed in the companies and the economy is certainly no richer, earnings per share are a third higher. On the strength of this showing, the market bids the new stock to an even higher multiple.

The stockholders rejoice. Remarkable! And in a way it is remarkable. For the increase occurs *even if A is not growing internally at all*. So long as A can buy a company with a lower p/e (and thus at a per-share price lower than its own valuation), it can raise the new company's earnings per share. And so long as the merged company, even if not growing, can keep on buying other companies with lower p/e ratios, even if *they* are not growing, its earnings per share will continue to rise. But the day inevitably comes when such a conglomerate runs out of acquisitions. Then, if there has been no internal growth in earnings, earnings per share will fall steeply. When that happens, the market price of the company's stock will probably fall even more as the growth expectations collapse. The stockholders who are in at the end are left holding the bag.

This version of the catastrophic possibilities in the chain-letter effect is based on a model set forth in the May-June 1968 issue of the *Financial Analysts Journal* by Marvin May, president of Tubular Structures Corp. of Los Angeles. In real life, of course, many conglomerates do show internal growth and try to buy companies showing internal growth. The ideal target is one with a lower p/e ratio than the acquirer *and* a higher rate of earnings growth too.

The fact that some conglomerates do try for internal growth reduces the likelihood of a catastrophic reckoning. But May points out that the investor buys permanent value *only* to the extent that growth in earnings per share is generated internally. When growth is entirely generated by acquisitions, the investor is playing a game of transfers or chain letters. When growth is partly internal, the situation becomes hard to analyze, but as long as companies buy others with lower price-earnings ratios, the combinations are bound to show a certain amount of false growth in reported earnings per share. And reported earnings are what the market looks at. Most purchasers of stock just don't take the time or trouble—or have the means—to separate apparent from real growth in an expanding conglomerate.

May concludes that *rate of growth in reported earnings per share is not an appropriate benchmark of growth for valuing mergers or acquisitions.* Several Wall Street financial men, including Robert Barbanell of Loeb, Rhoades & Co., are inclined to agree. What disturbs them all is that if the conglomerate movement keeps on expanding as it has been, a large percentage of values in the stock market will consist of conglomerate shares whose prices depend partly on false growth rates. Therefore they will be highly vulnerable to a revaluation; and since the market usually runs to extremes, swinging from overvaluation to undervaluation, the price-earnings multiple of conglomerate stocks could drop catastrophically. May is formulating guidelines on how to analyze conglomerate growth rates accurately, but Wall Street analysts are dubious about the venture. Many conglomerates have put their components together in such a way that it is almost impossible to pull them apart and make any sense of them. "They are in the earnings-per-share business, which defies analysis," says one analyst.

The Securities and Exchange Commission could compel conglomerates to account for their assets explicitly and consistently enough to judge true rates of earnings growth. But the SEC does not summarily order business to change accepted accounting methods. Its policy is to comment on a proposed ruling, throw the subject back to the accountants for "public exposure," and let the profession develop rules and regulations. The SEC is now, for example, trying to get diversified and conglomerate companies to report their operating results by divisions, and last year sent out a proposed ruling for comment. The Financial Executives Institute has protested most of the ruling, and the American Institute of Certified Public Accountants has taken issue with some of the provisions. What the SEC will ultimately do about divisional disclosure, and when, is yet unclear. But if this case is any guide, it will need a lot of time to persuade accountants to agree on a set of rules for judging the true growth of conglomerates. Congress conceivably may act, but probably not until the Federal Trade Commission's "study in depth" of conglomerates is completed.

Good Will Can Be Bad

The most popular method of accounting for conglomerate mergers also tends to value earnings per share inordinately and so to boost stock prices unduly. This pooling of interest probably accounted for only 30 percent of all mergers in 1965 but more than 60 percent in 1968. The reason for its popularity is clear when it is compared with the other principal way of accounting for mergers, the purchase method.

In a purchase, the acquiring company generally offers the target company cash or bonds or convertible debentures or some combination of these. (Cash requires no SEC registration.) One disadvantage of the purchase method is that the profits of the target-company shareholders are immediately taxable as capital gains. More important, accounting rules oblige the acquiring company to enter the assets of the target company in its own books at their current fair value. But when a company these days buys another with a lower price-earnings ratio, it almost invariably ends up by paying more than the target company's book value for its assets. Part of the difference between the target company's actual price and its book value must be charged to various assets and the rest to "intangibles" or some euphemism for good will. A conglomerate hates to show much good will because it suggests to analysts that the company has paid too much for the assets it bought.

Writing off good will cramps the style of a go-go conglomerator because good will is generally not tax deductible, and must come wholly out of earnings. Such a write-off reduces immediate reported earnings per share, and what the go-go conglomerator needs and craves is improvement in reported earnings per share, here and now.

The pooling-of-interest method, by contrast, involves paying in stock, either common or convertible preferred. It treats the companies' balance sheets as if they had always been combined, and simply adds up the assets and liabilities of both to get the totals. Until fairly recently this method was used mainly for what accountants call true marriages (as distinguished from acquisitions), in which companies of comparable earning power exchange stock at an agreed-upon ratio. A good example is the Penn Central union, in which neither the New York Central nor the Pennsylvania really acquired the other.

Aggressive conglomerators have found the pooling-of-interest arrangement very much to their taste. For one thing, an exchange of stock, whether the acquiring company offers its own common or new convertible preferred, does not generally oblige the target stockholders to pay capital-gains taxes until they sell the stock. More important, the profits of the target company are added to those of the acquiring company at once, boosting reported earnings for the year in which the deal takes place and perhaps conveniently papering over a poor performance by the acquiring company in that year. Most important, the good-will item is completely wiped out. When the two companies add up their assets and liabilities, they give no consideration at all to the fact that the acquiring company may have paid more than book value for the target shares, or that it has paid more than the market price. The value of the merged company's assets is understated and immediate earnings per share are overstated.

The accounting profession, appropriately enough, has been looking with increasing skepticism and even alarm at the latter-day use of the pooling-of-interest arrangement. Jacob S. Seidman of the C.P.A. firm of Seidman & Seidman, writing in *Barron's* last July 1, denounced the elimination of good will as a device for sweeping liabilities under the rug. He pointed out that, if the parent company sells underestimated assets at the price it paid for them, it is only recovering its cost, but can treat the difference between the price it obtains and the book value of the asset as a profit.

Two weeks later Abraham J. Briloff, professor of accountancy at the Baruch College of the City University of New York, named names. Briloff showed how Gulf & Western, during the year ending July 31, 1967, had issued some $185 million worth of securities with which it bought several companies including Paramount Pictures. Yet pooling of interest enabled Gulf & Western to record these acquisitions at their previous book value, which was less than $100 million. Briloff argues that this gave Gulf & Western a "submerged income pool" that it used to jack up earnings. In reckoning profits, that is, Gulf & Western didn't use the actual price paid for Paramount and other properties. "This means," Briloff goes on, "that G. & W. was able to generate income almost on a demand basis, without full corresponding costs being reflected in the income statement."

Even while such criticisms were being ventilated, George R. Catlett and Norman O. Olson, partners in the C.P.A. firm of Arthur Andersen & Co., were preparing a study on accounting for good will. The study, sponsored by the American Institute of Certified Public Accountants and released in October 1968, argued that the pooling-of-interest arrangement should be abolished. It is true that inflation and rising stockmarket prices have enormously increased the difference between the book value of a company's assets and the market value of its shares, and that the real difficulties in appraising the difference had driven many companies to pooling-of-interest accounting. Nevertheless, Catlett and Olson argued, "most business combinations, whether effected by the payment of cash or other property or by the issuance of stock, are purchase transactions and should be accounted for the same as other purchases." Assets acquired, Catlett and Olson concluded, should be recorded on the books of the acquiring company at fair value on the date of purchase, and the difference between the price paid and the fair value should be assigned to good will. Good will should then be accounted for as a reduction in stockholders' equity, and at the time of the combination.

Members of the A.I.C.P.A. committee sponsoring the study agreed that the pooling-of-interest arrangement is being abused, but they disagreed sharply on how to account for good will. J. S. Seidman, for example, was against writing it off against capital immediately, which the study recommended. Purchased good will, he argues, is nothing to be ashamed of, and should not be hidden or obliterated. So he suggests, somewhat sardonically, that the stigma attached to good will, a hangover from the days of watered stock, could be softened if the term were replaced with a phrase such as "premium paid for anticipated above-normal earnings." A skeptical analyst, gazing upon a huge asset entry thus labeled, might be prompted to add "on the assumption that the new management will produce higher earnings." A still more skeptical analyst might tack on "even when the new management knows less about the business than the old."

The SEC, which has already ruled that a current year's pooled earnings must not be compared with the acquiring company's earnings in previous years, is taking a vigorous interest in the pooling-of-interest controversy. But until the accounting profession itself comes to much closer agreement, it is hard to imagine the SEC's making a definite ruling about it.

Using the Target's Own Money

Even abolition of pooling-of-interest accounting would not be likely to brake the merger movement. Ingenious empire builders always find other effective ways to combine. Owing in part to the shortage of cash for purchases, more and more aggressor companies are discovering the advantages of buying other companies not with cash but with paper —i.e., with debentures (sometimes convertible), perhaps sweetened with warrants.

It is true that a target stockholder who exchanges his shares for debt securities must usually pay capital-gains tax on the immediate profit, but the acquiring company can offset this to a large extent by offering him a fat package. This is almost as easily done as said. In the words of George C. Demas, a New York City lawyer specializing in corporate take-overs, "A company takes over a company by using that company's own money. That is, the acquirer eventually pays off its I.O.U.s with the assets of the acquired company. In a sense, the weaker the acquiring company, the more it can offer, because dilution is no problem for it. Its important consideration is the assets of the company to be acquired."

Furthermore, the deal can be very profitable for the acquiring company even if it falls through. Suppose the stock of a rather languid company is selling at $70 a share and paying $4. Comes a raider offering a $90 convertible debenture paying $6, plus maybe some warrants to sweeten the pot. The raider times his offer so that the dividends on the shares he is tendered fall to him. These dividends then become inter-company dividends, which are 85 percent tax deductible; and the raider thus keeps about $3.40 of the $4. What is more, the $6 interest on the debentures he offers is a business expense and tax-deductible, and so costs less than $3. The raider, thanks to federal tax laws, makes more than 40 cents on each share tendered him, often more than enough to pay all expenses.

The big money, however, lies in quietly buying up nearly 10 percent of the target company's shares before making a tender offer (10 percent or more would require SEC registration), and then cashing in on the almost certain rise in the price of the stock. Some companies appear to have bought into other companies with no fixed intention of merging at all, but primarily to make money on the rise.

How the Loser Profits

Last April, Loew's Theatres Inc., a company with assets of only $250 million, put out a tender offer for Commercial Credit, a giant with assets of more than $3 billion. Commercial Credit was paying $1.80 a share, and its stock was selling at about $30. It was a self-satisfied asset-heavy outfit, but the stockholders seemed happy. Along came Chairman Laurence Tisch of Loew's, offering C.C. stockholders a $45 convertible debenture paying $2.475, and convertible to Loew's common at $90. Many C.C. stockholders rushed to take advantage of the offer. The interest, after taxes, cost Loew's no more than $1.25 per debenture, and the C.C. dividends, after taxes, brought it $1.65 a share. So Loew's made more than 40 cents on every C.C. share tendered. And the shares of both companies moved up sharply as traders, go-go funds, and arbitrageurs moved in. Loew's rose from around $70 to more than $100, and C.C. from around $30 to $55.

But Commercial Credit's management was apparently willing to unite with almost anybody to avoid uniting with Loew's. Luckily, Control Data, the ambitious computer manufacturer, was looking for just that kind of asset-rich, cash-heavy finance company. Control Data made an even richer offer than Loew's. Commercial Credit management backed it with hosannas of joy, and last June 16 the two companies reached an agreement to merge. Loew's appeared to have lost, but losing proved to be very rewarding. Before making the tender offer for Commercial Credit, Loew's had discreetly bought up 1,070,000 shares, nearly a tenth of the total outstanding, at an average price of around $30. Control Data's offer was good for about $65 a share. By the end of 1968, Loew's had realized a profit of $28,500,000, before taxes and expenses, on its $30-million investment, and it still held 5,300 shares of Control Data worth about $700,000. Its total profit on its non-take-over of Commercial Credit was nearly 50 percent greater than its 1968 net income from operations. Under the circumstances, discretion was manifestly at least as profitable as valor.

Gulf & Western probably did even better on its non-take-over of Sinclair Oil. The company picked up some 618,000 shares of Sinclair at an average price of less than $90. Although Sinclair shareholders elected to merge into Atlantic Richfield, Sinclair stock rose to more than $130 a share, and Gulf & Western came out way ahead. Gulf & Western finally settled by giving Atlantic Richfield an option to buy the 618,000 shares at $130, and in return got warrants to buy 618,000 shares of Atlantic Richfield, in the years 1970–76, at $125 a share. This could mean, according to one estimate, a profit of something like $50 million for Gulf & Western—compared to its 1968 reported profit of $69,800,000.

Sheer size of the target is no longer an obstacle to a paper take-over. A year or two ago, Wall Street jokers remarked that only General Motors and A.T.&T. were safe, but now some of the experts aren't so sure about G.M. "General Motors," argues one visionary financier, "is in many ways an ideal target. It has a low price-earnings ratio, relatively slow growth, large asset base, lots of cash, and high net worth. It is also shamefully underleveraged. Like Du Pont, from which it inherited its financial policies, G. M. has little debt. G.M. is thus practically a partner of the federal government, which takes more than half its gross profit. As a matter of fact, some have argued G.M. should have borrowed billions and bought in a lot of its own stock. This would both have raised earnings per share and provided leverage—would have enabled earnings per share to rise faster than earnings as a whole.

"Well, G. M. didn't take on a lot of debt. Now suppose some hero conglomerator printed up $15 billion worth of debentures and maybe another $10 billion in stock and warrants. G.M. stock, which pays $4.30, is selling at around $80. Our hero would offer, say, $125 worth of his securities, paying, say, $5 or $6 for every share of G.M. Once G.M. stockholders realized that I.O.U.s would really be paid out of G.M.'s own pocket, with the federal government footing part of the bill, they probably would trample over one another in the rush to exchange their shares. This may sound unthinkable. But things just as unthinkable are happening all the time."

The Kind of Value That Counts

No formidable obstacles seem to confront the conglomerate movement right now. Some conglomerate stocks have faltered, but the number of acquisitions has kept right on mounting. A major stock-market decline, as we have noted, might check the movement, but probably only for a while. And nothing in the way of immediate government intervention is likely to stop it. Chairman Emanuel Celler of the House Judiciary Committee has promised to investigate conglomerates this year. But the antitrust lawyers have not yet found a sure way of attacking them under present laws, and Congress isn't likely to frame a new law until the Federal Trade Commission's self-styled "study in depth" comes up with suggestions.

Quite apart from the possibilities of government intervention, a big question about conglomerates remains unanswered. That question has been well put by Dr. A. F. Rosenberg, president of Tyco Laboratories, a swiftly expanding high-technology outfit that Rosenberg aims to build into a large multi-market company. "The conglomerate movement has created market value," says Rosenberg. "Now can it create economic value?"

Can the conglomerates, to put it another way, make good in the marketplace? The question will take time to answer. The conglomerates' basic theoretical advantage is that they use capital more productively than ordinary companies. Thus they should elevate earnings on their own assets and, in the bargain, those of the economy as a whole. But this advantage is easier formulated than achieved, and a good many critics of conglomerates doubt that enough of them can achieve it to raise earnings on the assets of the whole economy very much. Some of the older companies like Textron and FMC have demonstrated that a multi-market company need not be dependent on the chain-letter effect for impressive earnings growth. But it will be several years before the later conglomerate creations will have had a fair chance to prove they are as good as they say they are.

Even if many conglomerates fail to increase earnings on assets, they may still be able to increase earnings on equity.

This they can do, as we have noted, by leveraging their capital—shunning new stock issues, buying up their own stock, assuming more debt, and otherwise reducing the proportion of equity in their capitalization. In the opinion of Warren E. Buffett, general partner of a highly regarded group of Omaha entrepreneurs called Buffett Partnership, Ltd., the "releveraging" of capital by conglomerates will be important enough to be described as a "real restructuring of American business."

There is something to be said for increasing the proportion of debt in corporate capitalizations. The policy of confining debt to a certain prudent ratio dates back to the time when business cycles were steep and sudden, and when all too often heavy fixed charges squeezed companies into bankruptcy. But today there is the corporate income tax, which roughly halves the cost of carrying debt. Today the country is committed to a policy of "full" employment, which in practice tends to be accompanied by considerable inflation—and one lesson of inflation is that going into debt to buy assets can be a way of acquiring them cheaply. Today some of the most respectable and even conservative corporations have successfully taken on relatively heavy debt loads, and glamorized their shares in the bargain.

Debt, nevertheless, has its hazards, particularly for a conglomerate whose year-to-year increases in reported earnings are in part dependent on the chain-letter effect of new acquisitions. Times might not have to get very tough or competitive for such a company to find itself looking desperately for hard cash or the equivalent thereof to satisfy its bondholders and keep its creditors at bay. Hard-pressed conglomerates might, for example, be forced to spin off some of their divisions. Given plenty of competition, the great conglomeration movement of the 1960s might conceivably be succeeded by the great deconglomeration movement of the 1970s.

Litton Down to Earth

THE CHEERLESS MEETING in the beige-carpeted, paneled conference room in Litton Industries' Beverly Hills headquarters lasted from noon until dusk on Sunday, January 21.
Present were five of Litton's top officers—Charles B. Thornton, chairman; Roy L. Ash, president; Glen McDaniel, chairman of the executive committee; Joseph T. Casey, vice
president, finance; and Ludwig Smith, senior vice president.
The question was how to tell the world that the company
was anticipating a decline in quarterly profits for the first
time in its fourteen-year history. Business was bad all right.
Several divisions in Litton's big business-equipment group
were in trouble. Moreover, top management had just discovered that the shipbuilding division needed to write off
$8 million of excess costs. In the New York and Boston
financial communities rumors were spreading that Litton
was in the grip of a serious management crisis, and the
stock was slipping. Something had to be said.

The five men agreed it was essential for any statement
to scotch rumors of a management crisis. They warned each
other that a badly worded announcement could lead to such
a headline as LITTON'S EARNINGS DROP CONFIRMS REPORTS
OF MANAGEMENT TROUBLES. This fear in mind, they spent
most of Sunday afternoon drafting a letter to stockholders.

109

Released the next day, the letter acknowledged that profits in the second fiscal quarter, due to end on January 31, would be "substantially lower than planned for this period." It conceded that the decline "is, to a great extent, the result of certain earlier deficiencies of management personnel." But, it added, "Organizational changes to correct this condition have been made."

Far from allaying any fears, the letter was taken by investors to mean that Litton—the very symbol of all that is modern in management—was indeed subject to seriously inadequate management. Matters got worse when Litton disclosed its actual results. Indicated net earnings for the quarter fell from $16,437,000 last year to $7,205,000, from 63 cents a share to 21 cents. This reduced per-share profit for the first half of fiscal 1968 by 30 percent from a year earlier. In the market Litton stock dropped eighteen points in one week. By early March, it was down nearly 50 percent from its 1967–68 high, $120.375. And the shares of other companies that many investors categorize as "Litton-like," e.g., Teledyne, Ling-Temco-Vought, Gulf & Western, also declined.

Litton's executives are still somewhat stunned by Wall Street's stern reaction to what they had considered reassuringly worded announcements. Thornton says of the earnings decline: "To us it's not anything. There were fifty-seven quarters when it didn't happen. Two, three, or four years from now, that one little dip in there will be practically meaningless." Adds Ash: "U.S. Steel was down 31 percent last year and there hasn't been all that much interest."

However, as Ash quickly acknowledges, a comparison of Litton's performance with U.S. Steel is beside the point. What made Litton an international legend, sent its price-earnings ratio into the stratosphere, and spawned droves of imitators was both rapid growth and, just as important, conviction on the part of investors that Litton's tirelessly enunciated concepts and management techniques had immunized the company against the ills that beset conventional corporations. Yet the picture of Litton's operations that emerged from the January letter and subsequent management attempts to explain things showed repeated and seemingly elementary mistakes in production, marketing, cost estimates, and pricing. Moreover, there was an apparent breakdown of Litton's vaunted system of internal forecasting and communication, under which every division's performance is measured at least once a month against detailed plans and projections. Management had not detected in advance the seriousness of problems in several divisions.

The Essence of Glamour

Predictably, there has been considerable gloating over the setback by cynics who had been presaging doom for all conglomerates through most of Litton's history; they have had a long wait. More surprising, however, is the contempt, even derision, that the nature of Litton's problems—and its managers' attempts to explain them—have aroused among some of its most sophisticated observers, the officers of other conglomerates. These people are particularly struck by the suggestion that management could be surprised in the closing weeks of a quarter by so many adverse developments.

There is a special incongruity about Litton's shortcomings. The men who run the company probably form as brilliant a group as can be found at the head of any corporation in the world. Their record of growth is almost unparalleled; in a decade, sales have shot from $83 million to a current annual rate of $1.8 billion. And the company has repeatedly demonstrated an ability to master the most advanced technology—to develop it, and to manage its application in enormous projects. Litton, for instance, originated and has since dominated the market for inertial-navigation systems used in manned military aircraft. And last year, by winning the design competition for the Navy's fast deployment logistics (F.D.L.) ship against competition from General Dynamics and Lockheed, it seemed to prove that it is superbly equipped to lead the transformation of the moribund United States shipbuilding industry. (Through no fault of Litton's, Congress has so far refused to provide funds for the $1-billion F.D.L. program.)

The essence of Litton's glamour has been the notion that its pioneering military technology, as well as the revolutionary managerial techniques needed to apply that technology successfully, could be transferred from federal projects to the comparatively hidebound world of private commerce and industry. But the requirements for profitability in government work are less exacting than those of the private marketplace. In the advanced government projects where Litton has made its special mark, success depends almost solely on performance. Barring flagrant mismanagement, the company that can do the job can be reasonably sure of clearing a respectable profit. Minor delays and mistakes of judgment can be overlooked, and contracts are drawn to allow for unforeseen snags in research and development. Private customers are less forgiving, largely because in most cases there are competing suppliers of roughly similar products. If products reach the market late, or if costs rise unexpectedly, sales and profits may be irrevocably lost.

Litton executives are not unaware of these realities. Their reason for shunning the description "conglomerate" (every conglomerate has at least one reason) is that the company, they say, has made its hundred or so acquisitions only in industries where its technological capability could give it a competitive edge. In truth, considerable mental agility is required to perceive an impending technological revolution in some of the businesses Litton has bought—e.g., office furniture. However, the company's plans for most of its divisions are convincing, and sometimes downright awe-inspiring.

Litton is relentlessly future-oriented; its executives find it more congenial to talk about how their companies will be operating five years from now than about what happened yesterday. However, technological revolutions take time. Meanwhile, the corporation is saddled with a fair number of everyday problems.

The origin of at least some of those problems is fairly clear. Several of Litton's important acquisitions, including Ingalls, the shipbuilder, Hewitt-Robins, a producer of materials-handling equipment, and Royal McBee, office machines, have been made at prices below book value. Although there are exceptions, sound, well-managed companies in growing industries are not normally available for less than their

book values. Other conglomerates rarely make such purchases. Litton has evidently been so sure of its ability to
transform the industries it has entered that the condition
of the companies at the time of purchase has been treated
as a matter of secondary importance.

Even before Thornton and Ash sent their extraordinary
letter to shareholders, there were signs that all was not well
at Litton. For years the company's net profit margin on
sales had hovered close to 4.5 percent. But in the final
quarter of the 1967 fiscal year, which ended last July 31,
the margin slipped to an indicated 3.6 percent. Costs above
planned levels in the advanced-marine-technology, office-
copier, and inertial-navigation divisions had trimmed over
$4 million from net earnings in one quarter.

In the next quarter, the first of the current fiscal year,
the margin on sales snapped back, but per-share earnings
were only 8 percent higher than a year earlier: 68 cents
against 63 cents. Last December, in its quarterly report, the
company tried to reassure the anxious. The 8 percent gain,
the report said, "becomes even more significant when measured against an average profit decline of 12 percent during
the period for the thirty companies comprising the Dow-
Jones industrial index. . . . Indeed, an important character-
istic of a multinational growth company is the capability to
maintain sound sales and earnings expansion through cyclical variations of the world economy."

Ash now says that the condition of the economy did
contribute to Litton's problems in the infamous second
quarter: "Neither Litton nor any other company totally
escapes the influence of outside factors. We don't exist outside the economy." Nevertheless, much of the problem was
strictly internal.

"The Need for Cost Control Developed"

One big factor in the decline, for example, was a series
of major civilian contracts on which the Ingalls shipyard
division had underestimated its costs. About half of Ingalls'
business is military—often, at least until recently, under
cost-plus-fee contracts. In those circumstances, explains
Harry J. Gray, a Litton executive vice president, "your

chances of losing money are not too great." In the first
years after Litton acquired the shipyard, its commercial contracts usually covered only one ship at a time; the chances
of calamities through inaccurate bidding were minimized.
It was only after big, multi-ship commercial contracts were
signed in 1964 and 1965, Gray says, that "the need for
cost control developed." When these controls were finally
instituted, Litton discovered that it had seriously underbid
on the contracts under which it is building fourteen auto-
mated commercial cargo liners for delivery this year and
next. The company now estimates that its costs will exceed the $200-million contract price by $8 million. Writing
off that loss in the second quarter reduced after-tax profits
by $4 million.

On top of that, trouble encountered by the business-
equipment group, which provides about a third of Litton's
sales, also had a serious effect on second-quarter profits.
Unexpectedly prolonged strikes at three of the group's plants
cost Litton some 30,000 lost man-weeks during the quarter.
But other setbacks suffered by this group would have been
enough to reduce the company's profit for the quarter even
if there had been no strikes. Difficulties cropped up in most
of the group's important divisions. Among them:

● Cole, a producer of low-cost metal office furniture. At
the end of 1966, Cole raised its prices an average of 28
percent to compensate for increased labor and material
costs. By last May, according to Harry Gray, it was clear
that the higher prices were seriously affecting Cole's sales.
Reduced volume pushed unit costs up further, but the
1,700-man work force was not trimmed. Gray, who replaced
William E. McKenna as head of the business-equipment
group last November, observes: "Management chose not to
see at that time the factors I have described, admittedly by
hindsight." However, Litton's corporate executives were in-
timately involved in Cole's decisions well before July, when
Cole reduced prices on a number of key items. The reductions failed to reverse the sales decline, though, partly because most users of Cole's catalogue were not aware of
them. By January, when revised catalogues reached customers, many buyers had already turned to Cole's competitors. Gray has written off several hundred thousand dollars

of slow-moving furniture inventory and reduced Cole's work force to 1,200 people.

● Monroe, which makes adding machines and calculators. In its January letter to shareholders Litton cited "volume variances from plan"—or, in plain English, disappointing sales—for Monroe calculators, as well as for Cole furniture. With Monroe, the problem seems to have been two-fold: first, the company was late in introducing electronic calculators, and second, it decided to enter the electronic-calculator market with a fairly sophisticated printing calculator, rather than a simpler display model. That decision has proved exactly wrong. Monroe's electronic printing calculators sell for about twice as much as electronic display machines. Consequently, buyers opted either for electronic display calculators or for conventional electric printing calculators.

● Royal Typewriter. Here the troubles centered on a new electric portable typewriter, designed to sell for considerably less than Royal's earlier electric portable. Litton acquired its design for the new portable in 1966, when it bought Willy Feiler, a West Berlin office-equipment maker. Royal wanted to produce the machines at its Dutch factory, but Feiler's design proved to need extensive engineering modification. Late in 1966, Litton bought Britain's Imperial Typewriter Ltd. and decided to transfer the portable to Imperial's plant at Hull. Confusion was loosed by the need to translate thousands of metric measurements into the British system; tooling for mass production of the portable was still going on last month. Royal's plans to have 100,000 of the portables on the U.S. market in time for Christmas 1967 went by the board. It now hopes to have the machines in the stores this summer. Meanwhile, to meet competition, Royal has had to offer volume discounts of 10 to 40 percent on its older, more expensive electric portable. "It's kind of tragic," Gray observes.

● Royfax, a producer of office copying machines. While Litton began making copiers in 1966, it has yet to capture much more than 1 percent of the market. Industry sources have long been skeptical of Litton's chances in the Xerox-dominated copier market, particularly since Litton's machines embody no radical innovations and use a less popular process that requires specially coated paper. Until recently, one of Litton's problems was that it produced only feed-through copiers. It planned to introduce a so-called "book copier"—similar in operation to Xerox's venerable 914—last June. But development hitches delayed the introduction until January.

Getting the Right Information

Ernest Stowell, a partner in the New York brokerage firm of Faulkner, Dawkins & Sullivan and an authority on the business-equipment industry, believes Litton's business-equipment group has been ill-starred for a long time—perhaps even since Litton entered the field with its acquisition of Monroe in 1958. He estimates the group's pretax profit margin on sales at 7 to 9 percent. By comparison, the average for the business-equipment industry is 20 percent.

Contrary to what might be expected from its record in other fields, Litton so far has rarely been at the forefront of business-machine technology. One reason, ironically, may have been an overemphasis on immediate profits. By tying managers' incentives to their current return on gross assets, Litton may have inadvertently discouraged them from spending enough on research and development.

In theory, Litton's system of management control should have revealed this problem. But there are inherent limitations to the amount of control Litton can exercise over its divisions. "Was management getting the right information?" asks Stowell. "My answer would be that they were not. Litton has very fine quantitative reporting techniques, but not qualitative. They must rely on their divisional managers to tell them that they are taking care of things qualitatively —whether they are keeping up with the field, with their customers' needs, with the technology."

In fact, Litton's top managers have been strongly implying that the information filtering up to them from the business-equipment group was misleading. Though they refuse to comment directly, it seems plain that the phrase "earlier deficiencies of management personnel" referred principally to Bill McKenna, who had been in charge of the group since 1964. McKenna, who was also a Litton director, left at the end of the first fiscal quarter—just before the deluge—to become president of Hunt Foods.

In his new office in suburban Fullerton, California, McKenna pointedly displays an effusive statement of thanks from Litton's board "to an esteemed friend and associate, William E. McKenna, for his outstanding services and contributions to Litton Industries." McKenna points out that the statement was presented to him only a few weeks before the letter to shareholders went out. He says he has no way of knowing what went wrong after he left. But he adds that the business-equipment group's profits were up 25 percent in fiscal 1967, and continued to meet planned goals in the first quarter of the current year.

The Murder Squad

McKenna's assessment of problems in his group may have been overoptimistic. But the whole point of Litton's system of constant, microscopic checking of the performance of its divisions is to see that corporate management quickly corrects any errors at lower levels. Operating managers submit monthly statements of their financial results and their progress toward previously agreed goals. In addition, at the beginning of each fiscal year each division has to produce a detailed plan and forecast of results for the coming year. The manager has to justify and defend his plan not only to the head of his group but also to what one former Litton man calls "the murder squad" of corporate executives, usually including Roy Ash. Once accepted by top management, plans must still be revised and updated every three months.

Because Litton uses this elaborate system of supervision, the phrasing of the letter to shareholders outraged many former employees. "How can they talk about 'earlier deficiencies of management personnel' when Tex [Thornton] and Roy are still there?" snaps one. Another says he has kept his last financial report to Litton's management, in case there is ever an effort to portray *him* as an "earlier deficiency."

Doubts raised by the recent troubles strike at the heart of Litton's concept of conglomerate management: the idea that talented general managers, applying modern management techniques, can effectively oversee diverse businesses in which they have no specific experience. Litton is still confident that the particular problems that caused the earnings decline are on the way to solution, and that its concept will prove itself in the future as it has in the past. "We do not want to change what we consider the right way to organize just because once in fifty-eight times something happened," says Thornton. "We will be more alert about the signals, but we won't change the way we operate."

Many people continue to think of Litton primarily as a defense contractor. However, for a number of years the company has been quite consciously shifting its emphasis from military to civilian business; currently, government work accounts for only a third of sales. The shift has broadened Litton's base, but it has also heightened the company's vulnerability to changes in the civilian economic climate. As Ash has implied, the tapering-off of the long boom in recent months accentuated the problems of Litton's commercial businesses. Because of its diversity, forecasts of Litton's course are particularly hazardous. A lot hinges on whether, and how soon, some of the company's exotic projects begin to produce significant sales and earnings.

Litton has an abundance of projects in hand that could pay off handsomely. Congress may yet revive the F.D.L. ship program. The company has submitted designs for the Navy's new landing helicopter assault ships, which could involve contracts worth over $1 billion. It has plans to offer an integrated ore-handling and shipping system to Great Lakes carriers. Ingalls expects to complete its highly advanced, $130-million shipyard at Pascagoula, Mississippi, by 1970. Litton has begun to get commercial orders for its inertial-navigation systems. And it stands to profit greatly if a mass market is ever developed for high-speed microwave cooking, in which it has pioneered.

A spectacular success in any one of these fields could offset, at least for a time, any continuing setbacks in existing operations. So could some big new acquisitions, though depressed prices for Litton stock could make some of these harder to bring off than in the past. The real question for Litton, however, is not just whether it can rebound from its current difficulties, but whether it can regain its former momentum. As Roy Ash says, "Litton today is not just a set of problems. There is no question in anybody's mind that Litton is going to be a successful large company. But our objective is to be a successful large *growth* company. We need to have a growth company, not only for our shareholders but for the people inside who provide our vitality."

Litton's own history has helped define tough standards for what constitutes a growth company. As it tries to meet these standards again, Litton will be operating under sharper scrutiny from investors, including some who used to accept its financial statements almost as divine manifestations. To revive its aura, the company will have to demonstrate, perhaps for the first time, that most glamorous of all corporate attributes—a consistent knack for earning high profits in commercial businesses.

Why Rain Fell
on "Automatic" Sprinkler

MANY CONGLOMERATE CORPORATIONS have had hard goings lately, but the one most battered by both internal catastrophe and stock-market reaction has been "Automatic" Sprinkler Corp. of America—a company whose history, even by the accelerated time standards of the conglomerates, has been so short and vertiginous that even its name is still only vaguely familiar to many businessmen. Based in Cleveland, Automatic Sprinkler produces such disparate items as electronic instruments, vacuum cleaners, bomb fins, hydraulic equipment, and baseball gloves, as well as sprinkler systems and other fire-protection devices. The quotation marks in its formal title are intended to distinguish its own automatic sprinklers from everybody else's and thus to protect the trade name. In late 1967, Harry E. Figgie Jr., Automatic Sprinkler's chairman and chief executive officer, was projecting earnings of at least $1.70 a share for 1967 and $2.75 a share for 1968; instead, the company was able to report only $1.43 in 1967 and 10 cents in 1968. Its shares —down from a January 1968 peak of $74, equal to fifty-two times earnings—have recently traded below $19.

The men who run conglomerates never tire of pointing out that their companies differ greatly from one another and that the experiences of one, either happy or unhappy, have little to do with those of the others. However, the troubles of Automatic Sprinkler have sprung less from the peculiarities of its product lines or corporate structure than from its status as a company growing explosively by means of multiple acquisitions in industries new to its management. It is worth looking at Automatic Sprinkler as a case history, for the pitfalls that it fell into threaten other conglomerates too.

Of course, in any corporate earnings decline as steep as Automatic Sprinkler's there is a large element of simple bad luck. But by its own actions, Automatic Sprinkler had placed itself in a position where luck had to play an unusually large part in its performance. Its growth rate for a while was exceptional, even for a conglomerate. Sales ballooned from $22,726,000 in 1963 to $325 million last year, primarily because of some twenty acquisitions. For the first few years profits rose even more dramatically than sales. Expectations that such a growth pattern could be sustained were fed by the company's hyperoptimistic projections of sales and earnings. To justify those projections, Automatic Sprinkler had to make mergers at a frantic clip. In the middle of 1967 four were completed in one twenty-five-day period. The pace was too fast to allow for thorough investigation of merger partners before deals were made, or for proper assimilation of newly acquired companies before management's attention was diverted to other negotiations.

Automatic Sprinkler officials have sometimes complained about the failure of conservative bankers to grasp the concepts of a growth company. But, in fact, until earnings slipped neither the company's directors nor the money market placed any effective barriers in the way of management's expansion plans. On the contrary, executives were encouraged in their course by some of the most sophisticated elements of the financial community. By the end of 1967, major mutual funds had bought up some 20 percent of the shares. Looking back to that time, the investment manager of one big fund recently observed with chagrin: "Of all the guys running conglomerates, Figgie of Automatic Sprinkler was the one guy that everybody thought really knew what he was doing."

Enough Size to Swing With

One of the things about Harry Figgie that most impresses fund managers, security analysts, and other such office-bound financial types is his easy familiarity with the nuts-and-bolts details of running a factory and cutting its costs. A large, bull-necked, tough-talking man of forty-five, Figgie does indeed have impressive credentials as an operating manager, though his background is far less proletarian than his appearance and manner suggest. The son of a onetime vice president of Rockwell Manufacturing Co., Figgie holds four academic degrees: two in engineering, one in law, and a master's degree in business administration from Harvard. He recalls that even as a teen-ager he had precise notions about his eventual career. "I made up my mind," he says, "that if ever I got the chance, I would put together a major U.S. corporation as Colonel Rockwell had done. So I started to plan my education and experience that way."

In 1953, Figgie joined the management-consultant firm of Booz, Allen & Hamilton. Six years later he was made a partner, and two years after that he became president of the firm's cost-cutting subsidiary, Booz, Allen Methods Service. In 1962 he left Booz, Allen in quest of some line operating experience and became a group vice president of A. O. Smith Corp. of Milwaukee, in charge of industrial products. In less than two years after he took over, the group doubled its sales and quintupled its profits.

Figgie never viewed A. O. Smith as more than a way station en route to taking over a company of his own, and by 1963, with things going well in the industrial-products group, he was actively looking around. His aim was to find a company with annual sales of around $20 million to serve as a base for a corporate empire. The reason for settling on the $20-million sales bracket seems to have been that companies in this size range were the biggest he thought he could raise the cash to acquire. With such a company, he has remarked, "you've got enough to swing with. A little company's got all the problems of a big company but less money, less time, and less talent to solve the problems."

Restricting his search to manufacturing industries, where

his experience had been concentrated, Figgie says he first looked at companies in such fields as laborsaving equipment, fluid controls, and instrumentation—all industries in which he has subsequently acquired positions. He soon heard about Automatic Sprinkler, and though fire protection was not a field he had been considering, he was immediately enthusiastic. The company, then privately held, had 1963 sales of $22,726,000 and net earnings of $334,000. Figgie, who has often proclaimed his belief that he can reduce the costs of virtually any industrial organization by 10 percent a year, saw ample opportunity to improve efficiency at Automatic.

When the company's owners expressed a need to close the deal before the end of 1963 for tax reasons, Figgie moved fast. The price was $5,851,156, some $1,376,000 less than the book value. He was able to raise the necessary cash in nineteen days, and on the last day of the year he became chairman of Automatic Sprinkler. His backers were a varied group whose common link seemed to be faith in Harry Figgie rather than excitement about the sprinkler trade. They included Cosmos Bank of Zurich and Laird & Co. of New York, each of which bought about a third of the original issue of common stock, and Saunders, Stiver & Co. of Cleveland, which took 13 percent. Shortly afterward these backers transferred about two-thirds of their common-stock holdings at cost to a larger group of private investors, including Bessemer Securities Corp. of New York.

Figgie swooped down on the leisurely operating practices of Automatic Sprinkler like a sort of business-school Billy Graham, preaching his fundamentalist gospel of cost reduction. The record he compiled in those first few months became a cornerstone of his credibility in the financial community. He made some savings by eliminating jobs and refining production methods, but his biggest initial coup came in the purchasing area. Having decided that the company was paying too much for raw materials, Figgie went to one major supplier and bluntly informed him that unless he dropped his prices by around 10 percent, Automatic Sprinkler would take its custom elsewhere. The supplier elected to meet Figgie's terms, making possible a $100,000 saving within a month of the change of ownership. During all of 1964, while sales rose a respectable but unspectacular 11 percent to $25,250,000, earnings more than tripled, to $1,188,000.

Those first-year gains were accomplished without making acquisitions, but by the beginning of 1965, Figgie was impatient to expand faster. Automatic Sprinkler took over four companies in 1965 and another four in 1966. The biggest of those acquisitions was American LaFrance of Elmira, New York, a producer of fire engines. Automatic Sprinkler's consolidated sales jumped to $45,877,000 in 1965 and $90,655,000 in 1966. In November 1965 the company went public; the corporate treasury and some of the original backers together offered about 20 percent of the common stock on the over-the-counter market. The offering price, adjusted for a subsequent split, was $7.80 a share, so even the recent depressed market for the stock has left early investors comfortably ahead. And since the price was about one hundred times the cost per share to the original backers in 1963 and 1964, the sale more than paid back *their* total investments. Underwriters for the offering were Saunders, Stiver & Co., which immediately prior to the offering held 74,500 common shares, and Laird & Co., which held 18,125, not counting those owned by a number of its executives. The remaining shares were held by the other original backers and the management. Figgie, his family, and Clark-Reliance, a company he owns, holds 299,526, or 4.4 percent of the total outstanding.

Most of Automatic Sprinkler's early acquisitions were connected with the fire-protection and construction industries, but some lay further afield. Kersey Manufacturing Co. of Bluefield, Virginia, a 1965 purchase, makes battery-powered tractors for use in coal mines. Hydraxtor Co. of Chicago, acquired in 1966, produces laundry equipment. These two companies were added to what Automatic Sprinkler pompously described as its "labor-reduction equipment nucleus."

Anyone who spends time around the head offices of conglomerates is likely to discover certain common strains of thought and expression among the executives encountered there. Almost every conglomerate manager agrees that the word "conglomerate" is totally misleading as a description of his own company but probably rather appropriate when applied to most of its counterparts. Such an executive will invariably stress that his own acquisitions conform to an intricate and farsighted master plan and an overriding philosophy of business, whereas, for all he knows, other corporations are opportunistically buying anything that comes down the pike. A pleasant literature of merger rationales has grown up, chiefly contained in the annual reports of these corporations, and Harry Figgie may well be its Shakespeare. His "Nucleus Theory of Growth," complete with an extremely scientific-looking diagram, was promulgated in the annual report for 1966, and has been detailed in subsequent reports, speeches, and even in a singular 33⅓-rpm phonograph record, mailed to shareholders, containing a six-minute exposition by Figgie.

The nucleus theory drew considerable attention to the company. During the 1966-67 academic year, for example, the University of Virginia's graduate school of business devoted much of its business-policy course to an extended study of Automatic Sprinkler. Professor Frederick S. Morton explained at the time: "We felt justified in using the Automatic series of cases because the growth of this company represents a conscious planned attempt to build a major corporation based on a specific conceptual framework and a fully defined business philosophy."

In truth, the nucleus theory, while reasonable enough, is neither as unique nor as scientifically rigorous as its presentation by the company made it seem. The theory hinges on the commonplace notion that optimum corporate growth can be achieved if acquisitions are made only in industries with above-average growth potential. The first acquisition in an industry is called a "nucleus." The company then attempts to acquire other firms in the same industry to group around the nucleus, eventually developing a corporate group of sufficient size to be a major competitive force in its industry. While mergers are going on, companies already acquired are subjected, according to the theory, to "a three-part program of cost reduction, sales and market expansion, and product research and development."

A Magic Touch—Twice

For all its formality, the nucleus theory has a lot in common with the rationales in general use among conglomerates. It posits no optimum corporate size and there is nothing in its internal logic to forbid the acquisition of any imaginable company in any industry, as long as growth potential can be claimed. It is true that the official diagrams, replete with lines purporting to show synergistic interplay among divisions, allowed for only six nuclei. But since one of the six was identified only as the "future growth nucleus," all options remained open.

As Automatic Sprinkler's acquisitions progressed, Figgie increasingly appeared to be acting on the belief that his talent for management made it safe to annex some companies with serious internal difficulties. The genesis of that belief was understandable enough. After nearly a decade as a consultant coaching other managers, Figgie had put his techniques and reputation on the line twice—at A. O. Smith and Automatic Sprinkler—and twice his touch had seemingly worked magic. Furthermore, at least one of his less robust early acquisitions for Automatic Sprinkler, Badger Fire Extinguisher Co., quickly became a reliable contributor to corporate profits.

To someone who is confident he can turn them around, companies with problems often look like bargains. However, even for a manager of Figgie's stature there is a big difference between concentrating full time on the problems of one medium-sized operation, as he had done before his acquisition program began, and putting out fires in many corners of a diverse corporate empire. In the experience of many merger-oriented companies, even subsidiaries that look perfectly healthy at the time of acquisition can turn out to have unsuspected weaknesses. Franc Ricciardi, chairman of the executive committee of Walter Kidde & Co., says emphatically: "It is *impossible* to know how sick a company is before you acquire it, and it is *impossible* to pay too little for a sick company."

During the period of Automatic Sprinkler's most rapid expansion, Figgie took a quite different view. He was fond in those days of asserting that he could gauge the condition of a company simply by walking through its plants. He ridiculed conventional yardsticks of value as "toilet paper," preferring instead to measure potential acquisitions almost exclusively by his judgment of how much they might contribute under his management to Automatic Sprinkler's future earnings per share. A fair number of the companies he acquired brought with them such problems as poor earnings, obsolete facilities, or unsettled labor relations. Moreover, few of the new subsidiaries had important proprietary products that could not be produced by competitors.

Conglomerates typically have very small corporate staffs; at Automatic Sprinkler the number of head-office executives is still only about thirty. It is humanly impossible for so compact a group to oversee the detailed operations of more than a small part of a multi-divisional company with sales in the hundreds of millions of dollars. To a certain extent, therefore, the benefits of having an operating expert at the top are dissipated as the company expands. Figgie prides himself on running Automatic Sprinkler as an operating company, rather than a financial edifice. But in any big conglomerate, whether management likes it or not, the main links between corporate headquarters and the divisions are necessarily financial. And the essential financial link is a reporting system that can be relied on to alert top management quickly to unusual occurrences at the divisional level.

Recognizing the necessity of such a reporting system, however, is a lot easier than setting it up. First of all, the accounting and other internal information-gathering methods of each division must be made compatible with those of the parent. This can be an arduous process in many newly acquired subsidiaries. Furthermore, even after a well-designed reporting system is inaugurated, its effectiveness depends largely on the competence of the divisional controllers who feed information into it. Ideally, these should be people of similar outlook and caliber to those on the parent company's financial staff. Such men are scarce, and not many of them are working for small and medium-sized companies; usually they have to be added to a subsidiary's staff after it is acquired.

The complexity of establishing a reasonably foolproof

financial reporting system is so daunting that even those who have struggled hardest with the problem, such as Litton Industries, have had notorious breakdowns. At Automatic Sprinkler, until the last year or so, there had been no serious, consistent effort to put such a system into operation. As a result, corporate management had to accept pretty much on faith such data as the divisions were able or willing to supply.

With his consulting background, Figgie must have been aware that potential disaster resided in this arrangement. Asked about it now, he concedes that the fast pace of acquisitions was partly responsible for the failure to forge better links to the divisions; management's attention was elsewhere. But he adds that some of the reluctance to make sudden changes was deliberate: "Our philosophy of management is retention of people. When you buy them, they are nervous. So we give them six months where you don't rattle the tree. You give them tremendous autonomy, especially in the first year. If we were in there too early, people would be flying out the windows."

A Report Too Good to Be True

Instead, profits flew out the windows. By the summer of 1967, a year in which eleven mergers were completed and sales jumped to $242,327,000, some unexpectedly grave problems were beginning to surface out in the divisions. The most worrisome were in the Powhatan Brass & Iron division of Ranson, West Virginia, whose products · include nozzles and other fittings for fire hoses. Under President Charles F. Reininger, who had been in the company since 1918, Powhatan had been maintaining excellent profit margins on sales that had grown from $2,681,000 in 1964, the year before it was acquired by Automatic Sprinkler, to $4,707,000 in 1966. But Powhatan's foundry was old and obsolete, and one of the reasons Reininger had sought a merger was Automatic Sprinkler's promise to supply the approximately $1,500,000 needed to build a new facility. Construction began soon after the merger, and the changeover from the old foundry to the new was being carried out during 1967. However, Reininger's health was failing, and visitors from the head office in Cleveland were noting by midyear that the installation of machinery and other start-up activities at the new foundry seemed to be taking longer than it should. "The hardest thing to set up is a new foundry," Figgie observes. "It is still state of the art."

When Powhatan's July report came in, however, it seemed too good to be true; the start-up delay was not reflected in the figures. Puzzled, Figgie sent some members of his financial staff from Cleveland to Ranson to find out what was going on, but they had no immediate success. "So much of the knowledge was in the mind of one man," Figgie says. "They had no standardized cost system, no product numbers even."

The mystery of Powhatan was particularly disturbing because there was little room in 1967 for slippage in divisions that were being counted on for profits. The company was facing factory start-up expenses in two other divisions as well. One of these, the Automatic Sprinkler division, was in the process of a relocation that added over $1 million to costs for the year. In January 1967, after its main plant in Youngstown, Ohio, had been closed for four months by a Teamster strike, the division decided to close it down. The manufacturing facilities were transferred to Georgia and the divisional headquarters to Broadview Heights, Ohio, near Cleveland. For almost all of 1967 the sprinkler division had to bus more than a hundred salaried employees from Youngstown to Broadview Heights, a daily round trip of 140 miles.

Top corporate managers had little time or energy to devote to the problems of Powhatan or other troubled divisions during the summer and fall of 1967. They were busy making mergers, including their first major contested acquisition: Interstate Engineering Corp. of Anaheim, California. Automatic Sprinkler first bid for the company at the beginning of 1967, but when Interstate announced its desire to merge with Beckman Instruments instead, Automatic temporarily withdrew its offer. In March, Automatic agreed to acquire Baifield Industries, a California ordnance company whose assets included 8 percent of Interstate's outstanding shares. Soon thereafter, Beckman's interest in Interstate waned. Negotiations between Automatic and Interstate reopened, and in late November the merger was completed.

For a lot of people on the outside, it was hard to see what Figgie wanted with companies like Baifield and Interstate, especially since the total Automatic Sprinkler shares given up for those acquisitions had a market value of almost twenty times those companies' recent earnings. Baifield was a metal-bending outfit producing rather mundane military hardware; its sales and earnings were completely tied to the national defense budget. Interstate had some interesting divisions producing such items as electronic equipment and camping gear, but 30 percent of the company's sales (which totaled $34,431,000 in fiscal 1967) and a huge 70 percent of its net income came from household vacuum cleaners, marketed under the brand name Compact.

These vacuum cleaners and another of Interstate's major product lines, Vanguard home fire-alarm systems, had been sold door to door by independent distributors. The sales pitch included strong emphasis on the promise that buyers could recoup $25 of the purchase price each time they put the salesman in touch with someone who subsequently also made a purchase. While most home vacuum cleaners sold in stores retail for less than $80, Interstate's machines cost around $200; an Automatic Sprinkler executive dryly observed not long ago that door-to-door selling is "an expensive method of distribution." As it happened, the proportion of customers who ever benefited from the rebate plan was slight, and in September 1967, after an adverse federal-court decision in New Hampshire and the implied threat of further action by the Federal Trade Commission, Interstate distributors abandoned this selling method.

Thus, at the very time it was making the final arrangements for the merger with Automatic Sprinkler, Interstate had to undertake a fundamental upheaval in its whole marketing program. Even though Interstate's reported earnings were already slipping before the merger, Automatic Sprinkler apparently accepted without question that Interstate was developing an alternative selling plan and anticipated no serious effect on sales and earnings. To avoid antagonizing Interstate's board of directors, which was not unanimous in endorsing the take-over, Automatic Sprinkler completed the merger without seeking any intimate knowledge of Interstate's operations. Moreover, Automatic Sprinkler failed to make payment in any way contingent on subsequent earnings. Quite plainly, the acquisition was one that the company was exceptionally anxious to bring off.

One reason for this eagerness may have been that Figgie had already publicly forecast Automatic Sprinkler's 1967 sales and earnings at a level that included the results of Interstate. Such predictions were nothing new for Figgie. Through 1966 and 1967 he had consistently assumed in his forecasts that pending acquisitions would be completed.

Figgie was particularly active as a prognosticator in November 1967. Automatic Sprinkler stock had been listed on the New York Stock Exchange in early October. Between mid-October and mid-November, its price slipped from around $57 to $45, partly because of rumors that the company was having internal difficulties. Some of the more garish rumors had it that Figgie had died. The company was sufficiently disturbed to call a number of breakfast and luncheon meetings with east-coast analysts and fund managers at which Figgie appeared, brandishing a letter from his doctor certifying that, apart from being overweight, he was in excellent condition.

At a special meeting of stockholders in mid-November, Figgie announced that Automatic Sprinkler normally expected to increase its per share earnings by 20 to 40 percent a year, and "should exceed the 40 percent figure this year." This indicated that earnings for 1967 would come to at least $1.61 a share. A few days later, Figgie was more specific. The year's earnings, he said, would be between $1.70 and $1.90 a share.

As late as the middle of January 1968, Figgie was still publicly confirming and even embellishing that estimate of 1967 earnings. Soon thereafter, though, as final audited reports of divisional results began to flow into Cleveland, the company fell silent. On Thursday morning, January 25, Figgie received figures showing that because of its marketing problems, newly acquired Interstate had performed disastrously. Its pretax profit had fallen from $5,197,000 in its last fiscal year before the acquisition to about $4 million in calendar 1967, with a lot of the drop having occurred in the last two months of the year. In December profit was only $34,741. Dale S. Coenen, a director who was in Figgie's office when that report arrived, recalls a scene of "utter disbelief." Explains Coenen: "We were sure that the operation was going to at least meet the [previous year's] earnings. It was cranked into our budget projections."

Any hope that unexpectedly good results in other divisions might help to offset the decline at Interstate flickered out in late January and early February. The news from Powhatan, where the auditors had at long last untangled the books, was dreadful. Costs connected with getting the new foundry on stream had indeed been much more severe than the division had admitted, and furthermore, Powhatan would have to write down a substantial portion of its metal inventory, which was overvalued. As a result, the division, which had earned $939,000 before tax in 1966, could report only $76,636 for 1967.

On Valentine's Day, Automatic Sprinkler announced its net earnings for 1967: $9,193,000, or $1.43 a share. This was an improvement from the $1.15 the company had reported a year earlier. However, it was not only below what Figgie had been predicting, but also down sharply from restated 1966 earnings of $1.75 a share. The restated figure includes past earnings of subsidiaries acquired in pooling-of-

Fast Rise, Fast Fall

Swelled by acquisitions, Automatic Sprinkler's sales have shot up more than 1,300 percent since 1963. Earnings were moving ahead briskly too, until the shocks of the past year and a half. Bad as the drop was in total net profits, it was even worse on a per-share basis: from $1.43 a share in 1967 to 10 cents in 1968. Earnings per share were whittled away by, among other things, an increase in common shares outstanding.

The leaps and dives of the stock price show how intensely Wall Street reacted to both the rapid growth and the setbacks. The chart traces monthly closing prices, adjusted for a five-for-two split in 1966. Of the two dozen big mutual funds that had bought into Automatic Sprinkler by the end of 1967, only one—Massachusetts Investors Growth Stock Fund—was still holding on in the spring of 1969; it had some 200,000 shares. That fund's paper loss on the stock: about $6 million.

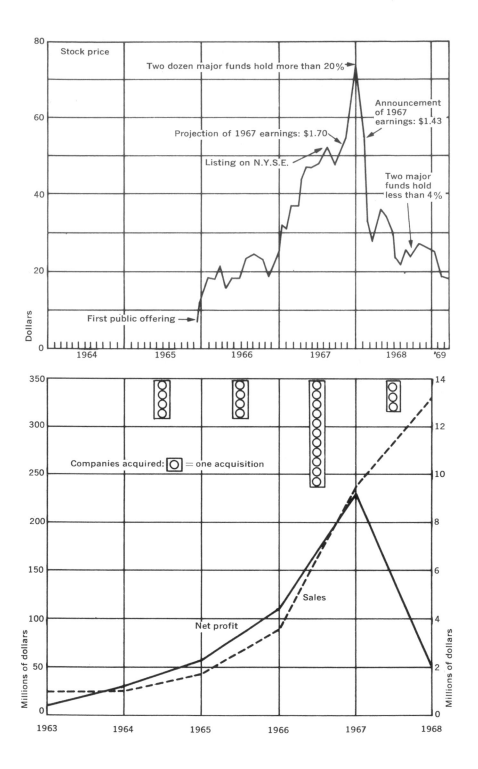

interest transactions during 1967, e.g., Interstate. Since that earnings announcement, Figgie has become harshly critical of the accounting requirement that past earnings be restated in this way, alleging that it makes for misleading comparisons. However, he remains an enthusiast of other aspects of pooling-of-interest accounting, such as its provision for incorporating into the most recent year's results the earnings of companies acquired after the end of the year but before the publication of the annual report.

Not surprisingly, many of the analysts and investors who had acted on the basis of Figgie's November and January predictions regarded the failure to produce the promised earnings as almost a betrayal, and there was a massive sell-off of the company's stock. Mutual funds were prominent among the sellers. Of the two dozen major funds that owned the stock at the beginning of 1968, only one was still hanging on this spring. For some reason, Automatic Sprinkler evidently was unprepared for this outbreak of what one incredulous former executive remembers as "so much emotion."

Confusion over what was going on inside the company was compounded by the official explanation that accompanied the earnings release. Although it mentioned Interstate's problems and alluded to Powhatan's, the statement ascribed the earnings discrepancy largely to two other factors. One of these was the relocation of the Youngstown operations. Since that move was initiated in the first month of 1967, however, it was hard to see how its costs could have surprised management a full year later. Figgie now agrees that most of those costs were known when he made his projections.

The other difficulty that Automatic Sprinkler pointed to was a delay in a planned merger with George J. Meyer Manufacturing Co., a family-controlled maker of automatic packaging and bottling equipment and materials-handling systems with 1967 sales of $63 million. But Figgie now says the best figures he had through mid-January 1968 showed that earnings would reach $1.70 a share without Meyer, or $1.86 a share with Meyer. Thus, whether Figgie did or did not originally specify that his projection included Meyer

—a question that has become a bone of contention between the company and its critics—is, by Figgie's account, irrelevant.

Automatic Sprinkler first approached Meyer only on November 25, 1967, so there was no realistic hope that it could be acquired before the end of the year. However, Automatic Sprinkler did expect to complete the merger early enough in 1968 to pool its 1967 figures with those of Meyer. This plan hit a snag when Automatic Sprinkler's stock price plummeted in January and February. The drop meant that the company had to give up 64 percent more shares than it had planned in its exchange with Meyer. Issuing the new shares caused the delay, and the dilution torpedoed previous estimates of Meyer's initial earnings contribution. Based on the exchange formula under which the merger was finally completed in late March, Meyer would have added only 2 cents a share to Automatic Sprinkler's 1967 earnings.

His Ultimate Accolade

Upsetting as they were, the difficulties of 1967 were only a mild prelude to the catastrophe of 1968, when profit fell to $2,121,000, or 10 cents a share. Some of the problems were just carry-overs from the previous year. Powhatan continued to have trouble with its new foundry, and Interstate's vacuum-cleaner sales continued to lag. In addition, Interstate's electronics division, previously one of its stronger units, took a substantial loss on a fixed-price contract to supply in-flight maintenance equipment for the Air Force's C-5A cargo plane.

By far the most important factor in the 1968 decline, though, was Baifield Industries, the California defense contractor that had been so helpful in Automatic Sprinkler's pursuit of Interstate. Before the acquisition, Baifield had signed a $6,271,000 government contract to produce casings for 105-millimeter armor-piercing shells. During 1968, Baifield took a staggering $8-million pretax loss on that contract. The write-off included all anticipated losses through the contract's scheduled completion. As Automatic Sprinkler people explain it, Baifield underbid on the contract, assumed an obligation to use untested equipment supplied by the government, and accepted delivery on a large quantity of steel that proved inadequate to meet specifications.

The cave-in at Baifield was particularly galling, for at the time of the acquisition that company had seemed to be in excellent shape. Thinking back to an early inspection tour of Baifield's main plant with Leonard Barbee, Automatic Sprinkler's vice president for manufacturing, Figgie remembers dispensing his ultimate accolade. "I couldn't spot a single method improvement," he says. "Barbee could only spot two. So it was a pretty well-run company." James Upfield, Baifield's president, is described by Figgie as "a tool and die maker with a fantastic record of accomplishment. Probably what happened was he had too many bases to cover and didn't have time to oversee every detail."

For a long time Baifield just could not turn out casings of acceptable quality; but even though losses were mounting, there was no possibility of simply abandoning the contract: one does not quit on one's only customer. Last summer Upfield resigned as president and was replaced by Daniel L. Watters, who had been vice president for finance and administration. There are hopes that Baifield will break even this year, which would be an improvement over 1968 but still nothing to cheer about. In its last fiscal year before being acquired, Baifield had a net profit of $1,763,000.

On top of these setbacks, Automatic Sprinkler also suffered from the kind of mundane business problems that would hardly be noticed in a good year but add to the crisis of a bad one. Like other highly leveraged companies, it was hit hard by rising interest rates last year. Because the interest rate on some of its bank loans fluctuates with the prime rate, each one-point rise in the prime rate reduces Automatic Sprinkler's net earnings by about 5 cents a share (even apart from the added costs of refinancing fixed-interest debt at increased rates). Also, two divisions suffered lengthy strikes, another had to write off several hundred thousand dollars in bad debts, and still another, which makes truck-mounted concrete mixers, experienced a steep sales decline after the government placed an excise tax on mixers of that kind.

Automatic Sprinkler's acquisition program has been more

or less stalled since the collapse of its stock price last year. Aside from Meyer, only two small acquisitions were completed during 1968. Through most of 1968, Automatic waged a vain struggle to take over U.S. Pipe & Foundry Co.; last month it agreed in principle to sell its 23.7-percent holding in U.S. Pipe to Jim Walter Corp. for about $32 million. Automatic Sprinkler has taken advantage of the respite from its previous frenzy of mergers to institute some much-needed internal structural reforms. The most significant move was the appointment last September of James H. Goss, sixty-one, as president and chief operating officer. Goss, a courtly, restrained man whose style nicely offsets Figgie's ebullience, had retired from General Electric after a distinguished thirty-seven-year career that gave him plenty of practice in managerial rescue work. At various times he headed—and engineered profit turnarounds in—G.E.'s international, Canadian, and consumer-goods operations. "I've been in trouble spots all my life," he says.

Under Goss, the organization of subsidiaries into rational corporate groupings has been speeded up. There are now five group vice presidents, all drawn from the divisions, and the companies that make up the groups have been rearranged into twenty-five operating units. This has involved combining some acquired companies and splitting others, such as Interstate, into a number of parts. One recent consolidation brought together Blaze Guard, which makes hoses, Powhatan, and Badger Fire Extinguisher. Though all three companies sold to fire-safety distributors, Powhatan and Blaze Guard had no full-time salesmen in the field, while Badger's nine-man sales force covered three-quarters of the country. Now all three will benefit from that sales force.

As chairman, Figgie retains responsibility for the administrative staff and the merger program. He has added more than a dozen men to the corporate financial department, and head-office auditors patrol the divisions. The previous financial vice president, James J. Gilligan, resigned a year ago and now heads a Philadelphia construction-supply company with ambitions of becoming a conglomerate.

Odd as it may sound to investors who once thrilled to his talk of 20 to 40 percent annual profit gains, Figgie seems genuinely surprised that anyone should so lack historical perspective as to be upset by short-term corporate reverses. "We're playing this ball game for the long run," he says earnestly. "This is my life's work and, God willing, I've got twenty-five years. We'll be a blue chip someday."

Right now, though, the company still has smoldering problems. A number of important divisions remain in questionable health. The internal changes being made do seem to be repairing some of Automatic Sprinkler's most glaring organizational deficiencies, and the company is strengthened by having several divisions that have continued to perform excellently despite the corporate bombshells detonating around them. Still, the management remains very far from winning back the confidence of institutional investors. Many financial men are waiting to see whether Figgie and Goss can come up with record 1969 sales and earnings, exclusive of any new acquisitions. It is widely felt that nothing less would be convincing evidence of a turnaround at Automatic Sprinkler.

PART III

Offense
and Defense

How to Fend Off
a Take-over

PRACTICALLY EVERY SIZABLE U.S. corporation, whether it realizes it or not, is under scrutiny by some other corporation as a prospective acquisition. But probably nine out of ten prospects, for a wide variety of reasons, don't want to be taken over by the people who would like to take them over. What should the unwilling targets do?

The first thing they should do, the experts agree, is to study the strategy and tactics of present-day corporate take-over artists. The raider begins by taking a lot of trouble to familiarize himself with his target—who holds the stock and where, whether it is in strong hands, and what its trading pattern has been. He also gives special attention to what might be called the human vulnerabilities in the company. According to Stanley Sauerhaft and Richard Cheney, Hill & Knowlton vice presidents specializing in the public-relations problems of take-overs, the raider does not confine himself to ordinary personnel research jobs. He compiles dossiers on the managers, complete with everything from their stockholdings and past deals to their personal grudges and weaknesses. He sometimes uses all the classic devices of industrial espionage, from wiretapping to downright bribery. One way he helps get things lined up is by ferreting out and making an ally of a disgruntled target-company officer.

At the same time, the raider probably is buying stock of the target company. Since his take-over attempt will be most effective if it comes as a complete surprise, he picks up shares over the course of weeks and even months, trying to avoid pushing up the price. Except for two or three of his top officers, he lets no one in on his plans, and takes elaborate steps to make sure no word leaks out. One raider made his treasurer personally examine every piece of paper in executive wastebaskets at the end of the day. Whether that had anything to do with it or not, the impending take-over was successful.

If the raider has enough money or can borrow enough, he tries to accumulate just under 10 percent of the target company's stock—which he can do without having to register with the SEC. With that much stock, he is better equipped to have his way with management, which usually owns much less. Armed with a hefty holding of target-company stock, the raider suddenly calls on the company's chief executive and breaks the good news, explaining how the proposed take-over will be in the best interests of management, company, industry, and the whole economy. Often the explanation is made more convincing by the raider's observation that the compensation of the target company's executives seems rather meager. But if the target executives still say no or stall for time, the aggressor moves fast. He demands a list of the target company's stockholders, plasters the papers with advertisements proclaiming his fabulous offer, and launches well-prepared public-relations campaigns in cities and towns where the target company is important. He may drop a few words ahead of time to the go-go funds, which then buy a lot of the target company's stock from shareholders who are willing or anxious to settle for a nice quick profit. Later the funds tender the stock to the raider at a nice quick profit for themselves.

Such is the art and science of the modern corporate raider. Obviously enough, no target company, no matter how mighty, good, or great, can afford to dismiss the possibility that it may be taken over. If it doesn't want to be absorbed summarily, it must prepare itself in advance. To begin with, it must accept the fact that a new era has dawned for the long-neglected stockholder, who as a rule can be expected to sell out to the highest bidder. It does a target company little good, says Cheney, to denounce the raider as a horse thief. The mere possibility that a horse thief will take over his company makes the stockholder all the more anxious to sell at a profit. Nor does it do much good to tell the individual stockholder with a fat immediate profit that the deal will prejudice the long-term interests of stockholders as a group. He'll put his own short-term interests first. As a matter of fact, target companies cannot depend even on what they have always regarded as bastions of strength, the stock held in trust by institutions. Last year, for example, one Baltimore bank calmly sold most of its holdings of Commercial Credit when Loew's tried to take over C.C.

The target company would also do well to realize that the most effective defenses against take-overs amount to adopting some of the raider's own notions about corporate organization. Raiders, for example, prefer not to attack a well-leveraged company—that is, one with a relatively large proportion of debt in its capitalization. Although it may be late for a low-debt corporation to restructure its capitalization formally, it can resort to the simple stratagem of buying in its own stock with debentures. If its own shares are selling at $60, for example, it can offer its shareholders debentures worth perhaps $80 or even $90. This would not only put off raiders, but might reduce the cost of servicing the company's capital by substituting tax-deductible interest for nondeductible dividends.

Such a countermeasure, however, is as yet unpopular. Aside from the fact that it might raise the SEC's eyebrows, it runs counter to conservative financial policies; to many a treasurer it is just another manifestation of the irresponsibility that afflicts the whole country in 1969 A.D. "And this is why corporations on the defense side often have the wrong people fighting a take-over situation," comments Edward Dugan Jr. of Smith, Barney & Co. "We try to tell them that if they are worth more to the other fellow than in the marketplace, there is little they can do about it except find a more compatible partner or start buying companies themselves."

One less convulsive way for a potential target company to discourage if not forfend a take-over is to improve its profit performance and hence the market price of its shares. This, likewise, cannot ordinarily be done overnight. But it is never too late to become ostentatiously interested in new products with a touch of glamour, and the easiest way of doing so is to shop around for a company or two of the kind associated with swift growth. There are also ways of making profits *look* better very quickly. One is to change bookkeeping practices. Ever since Jimmy Ling bought a controlling interest in Jones & Laughlin, several steel companies have switched from the accelerated-depreciation accounting to the straight-line method, which, though it does nothing for cash flow, brings more money down to current net income.

Most of the other means of fighting take-overs fall under the heading of tactics rather than strategy. The target company might suddenly split its stock; since an aggressor must usually offer a higher premium for low-priced than for high-priced shares, this might discourage him. The target company might merge with or take over a company that competes with the aggressor; although such an acquisition may improve the target's own prospects little, it automatically puts antitrust law in the way of the proposed take-over. Or it might buy several small companies, thus getting more of the stock into friendly hands and at the same time increase the "float" or amount of stock outstanding. Or it might build up friendly stock ownership by such devices as restricted stock-purchase plans for its executives.

The rest of the tactics, for the most part, consist of obvious but often overlooked steps that are the stock-in-trade of take-over lawyers and public-relations experts. The target company should:

● Analyze its stockholder list by size of holdings, area, types of ownership; using this information, it should try to spot any extraordinary accumulation of the stock.

● Change its bylaws so that a meeting cannot be called unless, say, two-thirds of the stockholders are represented.

● Be careful not to raise the percentage of stockholder votes needed to ratify a merger too high; doing so may defeat a preventive merger.

● Call in attorneys, public-relations men, and proxy soliciting organizations as soon as it feels it will be attacked.

● Be prepared to tell stockholders a lot it may not have told them before, including information about hidden assets that may help turn the company around.

● Contact its stockholders; arrange to see the big ones personally, and prepare letters complete with stamped envelopes for the rest. Also prepare stand-by telegrams and press releases.

Probably the neatest recent repulse of a raider, however, involved none of these devices. The target was Magnetics, Inc., a small Pennsylvania company making alloys and magnetic components. Last fall, Hale Brothers Associates of San Francisco apparently decided that Magnetics would be an excellent vehicle for building a conglomerate, and offered to buy 65 percent of the stock at a 30 percent premium. The offer looked like a sure thing for Hale Brothers, but Arthur O. Black, president of Magnetics, was undaunted. He and his top officers simply threatened to resign and start a new company making the same products as Magnetics. Neither Hale Brothers nor Magnetics stockholders could do anything about it. To the observation that his unilateral action might open him to a stockholders' suit, Black simply replies that the Civil War was fought to guarantee Americans against involuntary servitude.

The case of Magnetics, however, is just about unique. Take-over experts agree that it would be neither useful nor prudent for the top executives of steel, auto, or insurance companies to threaten to resign. Some raider might take them up on their offer.

United Fruit's Shotgun Marriage

AFTER A SEASON of pursuit by some of the liveliest operators in the field of corporate aggrandizement, United Fruit Co., the Boston-based banana empire, finally went to AMK Corp., the swelling creature of Eli M. Black. Once Black made his interest apparent last fall, there was little doubt that United Fruit's management would lose control to someone. Flopping around desperately in an effort to get away from Black, United Fruit tried to make itself very attractive to a couple of other suitors. But Black had laid his plans too well. And now the venerable, asset-laden concern is his.

It may be a little early to decide just how good a deal the acquisition will turn out to be in the long run. But up to this point, anyway, it's a good deal for just about everybody concerned: the small as well as the large stockholders of United Fruit, the brokerage firm that first brought the prospect to Black, the other brokers who profited by the churning markets in the securities of AMK and United Fruit, and the commercial bankers who lent Black the money to buy the company. Even United Fruit's executives have come through largely unscathed: some feelings were bruised and managerial powers lost, but with little dislocation they will be able to keep on doing what they have done best— grow bananas and bring them to market. The other com-

146

panies that made their passes at United Fruit lost almost nothing but face when their efforts proved fruitless. As for AMK itself, no one knows yet what Black will do with United Fruit's untapped resources, but he picked up plenty of them to tap.

The AMK-United deal grew inevitably out of the two disparate approaches that now prevail in American business life. One stresses operations, the other asset management. For sometime before it fell to AMK, United Fruit had been displaying a pair of attractions only a little less prominent than those of that celebrated lady who stopped traffic in New York's financial district. The twin appeals were the absence of any funded debt, and around $100 million in cash. The company's top management knew well what it had, and knew that it ought to put those assets to work for its shareholders. But neither John M. Fox, chairman and chief executive, nor Herbert C. Cornuelle, president, was able to come close to using their money and borrowing power—easily $300 million—in the way that counted: making significant acquisitions.

Yet these are men who effected a major turnaround in the fortunes of their company. They brought sales last year to a record $509,500,000, with per-share earnings of $3.80—down from $4 in 1967, but still higher than any year since 1955. Both men had been aggressive and successful promoters for major food processors before coming to Boston. But those were *operational* accomplishments—the accomplishments of men who limited their vision of what their company could do to what it and they had already done well before.

Eli Black looks at things differently. He won't be strapped by any inhibitions about the "right fit" of products or geography. He is an asset manager, and whether he knows a banana tree from a potted palm is largely irrelevant. His ability lies in uncovering value on a large scale, getting control of it, and putting it to work uncovering more assets. While United Fruit's people were putting their banana business in order and buying a few little things here and there, Black was taking a group of unexciting manufacturing units, with the unexciting name of American Seal-Kap Corp., and turning it into AMK, a taut machinery maker doing around

$40 million a year. He vaunted into the limelight when he acquired a company twenty times bigger: John Morrell & Co., a meatpacker grossing $800 million annually.

After that coup, an operating man would have immediately turned his attention to tightening up Morrell, and fitting it into the parent structure. But not Black. He leaves problems like that to others. In fact, he was just weighing the takeover of Great American Holding Corp., an insurance complex, when the United Fruit deal was brought to his attention. Few men have ever been more pleased to be interrupted. Black grabbed the opportunity, knowing for sure from the start that he would find plenty to do with the assets he wanted. He was just a jump ahead of others with the same assurance—and intentions.

In the long run, as more and more managers of assets come into the market, bidding up the treasures buried in balance sheets, prices may go too high. Even "Chinese money," the convertible subordinated debentures that have been used lately for tenders of stock, bears interest that must be earned and paid. The operations men may come back into favor another day. But in the short run, Eli Black will be riding high as he looks for high-yield investments for his new bundle of assets. His recent purchase of a major holding in Long Island's Security National Bank shows one direction he can be expected to take. There are sure to be others.

The Merger Makers

As an established acquirer, Black was a logical prospect for the brokerage firm of Donaldson, Lufkin & Jenrette, when it decided to take a group of its customers out of United Fruit's stock last year. Their portfolios contained enough of the company's stock to give any single buyer a big headstart toward control.

In making the deal, Black departed from his usual method. Before he bought a single share of Morrell's stock, he talked at length with the company's officers. Black says he would have preferred to approach United Fruit first too. But the word was already out that someone else was about to ask for tenders. And there was the powerful magnet of that clean balance sheet. So Black skipped the formalities that he usually puts so much store by. He bought the block of stock, and talked afterward.

On Tuesday, September 24, the New York Stock Exchange ticker reported a trade of 733,200 shares of United Fruit's stock at $56, more than $4 above the market price. In shares and dollars, it was the third-largest block ever traded on the Exchange up to that time. Though the buyer was not publicly identified at the time, it was AMK. On the same day the company bought another 7,100 shares in the open market, giving it a total of 740,300 shares, or more than 9 percent of the total stock outstanding. To finance the bulk of his purchase, which cost $41,778,000, Black borrowed $35 million from a group of banks headed by Morgan Guaranty Trust Co. Besides the $56 a share, Black offered the owners of the block another inducement: he proposed that if he decided to ask for tenders, he would allow the former owners of those 733,200 shares to return AMK's money and accept instead the package of AMK securities he would offer. They all eventually did just that.

Black also found an appropriate way to express his gratitude to Donaldson, Lufkin & Jenrette. In addition to the $327,000 in commissions that the firm was entitled to from both buyer and sellers in the transaction, Donaldson, Lufkin is to get a fee that may run to $1 million. That constitutes recognition that the firm did more than just act as broker. It knew where the stock was, and it was able to pry loose a block of shares big enough to give Black not only nearly 10 percent of the equity but the advantage of surprise as well. And Donaldson, Lufkin did well for those of its customers who were shareholders in United Fruit but were not sellers at the time: the very fact that so big a block had passed into the hands of a noted collector of companies all but guaranteed a sudden revival of interest in United Fruit. That in itself would move the price of the stock even higher. The firm's clients who held on to their shares could get out with a profit later on.

Donaldson, Lufkin & Jenrette is a Stock Exchange firm formed by eager young men who specialize in institutional customers, including mutual funds. It also does a big investment-counseling business, managing hundreds of millions of dollars worth of accounts. During 1967, William Donaldson had recommended to many of these customers that they buy United Fruit, which had fallen out of favor earlier because of some years of disastrously poor earnings. (At least two major funds, Dreyfus and Affiliated, had made major investments in United stock some time earlier. In fact, Affiliated had the largest recorded position, with 300,000 of the eight million shares, mostly bought in at around $20.) Explaining his firm's recommendation to buy shares in a company that had been through such troubled times, Donaldson says, "There had been a rapid increase of institutional interest in United during 1967. People were beginning to have faith again. The risk-reward opportunities looked great. But when you have a company with earnings like United Fruit's in 1958–64, you make sure that the direction is clearly up, and that you see a permanent improvement."

Although by 1967 United Fruit had recovered from a series of disasters, the market had already pretty much discounted that recovery. The price passed $60 in the last quarter of 1967 ("overexpectation," said Donaldson), but by July 1968 it was down below $50 ("the dock strike and out-of-proportion disillusionment"). So Donaldson looked for a buyer to get his customers off the hook.

Obviously, at $56 a share, there was more United Fruit stock to be had, but by buying just less than 10 percent, Black avoided becoming an insider under SEC regulations. Otherwise he would have had to report his trades and would have been prohibited from taking short-term profits —an option he wanted to leave open in case he changed his mind about acquiring the company. "We felt that the purchase had to be sound in its own right," says Black. "If nothing more happened, this had to make sense. We felt it did. The stock was purchased at thirteen times earnings, and the company's balance sheet was extremely conservative. So our risk on the downside was very limited. Even if nothing further happened, we would probably have ended up selling it at a substantial profit."

As it turned out, other companies would have been happy to buy United Fruit's shares from AMK, and a couple tried. But Black wasn't selling. When others attempted to get control of United Fruit for themselves, Black remained supremely confident. The fact that he held nearly 10 percent of the shares accounted for much of that confidence. The likelihood that he could get another 10 percent from Donaldson, Lufkin sources gave him more confidence still. Black could therefore enter any struggle for tenders with something like 20 percent of the company's stock already sewed up. In such a struggle, any competitor for the company would have to pick up more than 50 percent of the voting shares. Black would have needed only just over 30 percent.

The Treed Fox

The way John Fox of United Fruit first heard about the AMK transaction reveals a lot about his view of his function. Chief executives of aggressive, asset-oriented companies commonly get hourly reports of prices of their company's shares and the volume changing hands. But Fox first heard about AMK's huge purchase when Donaldson's office called him. "They wanted me to meet the new stockholder," Fox recalls, "but they wouldn't say who it was. Then I got calls from the Morgan Guaranty and Goldman, Sachs. They all had the same story: he's a nice guy, etc., but they wouldn't give his name." When he was finally contacted by Black, Fox agreed to have dinner with him that evening in Boston. It must have been a pretty hard meal to digest. "Black told us," Fox says, "that he saw a lot of synergy in a mix of the two companies, but that he didn't want to do any more without our agreement. Our reaction was that we didn't know anything about AMK, and that we could run our own company."

Fox made a couple of efforts to withstand the AMK assault. He turned first to Dillingham Corp., the Hawaiian contractor and real-estate developer. Then he solicited Textron, Inc., the New England conglomerate. Both companies made offers, but they faced earnings dilution and were apprehensive about United Fruit's heavy foreign investment. And Black's grip was too firm to be shaken.

Just from a look at United Fruit's history, Fox could have seen its vulnerability. Back in 1933 the management had been taken over by a former competitor, Samuel Zemurray. He had sold out to United Fruit, became its largest stockholder, and then taken control. He too sought to invest more productively those assets that the staid heirs of a once-lusty company had protected, but not used, during the depths of the depression.

But even if Fox hadn't read that particular chapter, he might have done better in his recent predicament. For one thing, he could have got sophisticated help from at least three members of his board. They included George Peabody Gardner Jr., descendant of two ancient Beacon Hill families, chairman of United Fruit's executive committee, and a general partner in the firm of Paine, Webber, Jackson & Curtis; Stanley de J. Osborne, former chairman of an early conglomerate, Olin Mathieson Chemical Corp., and a general partner in Lazard Frères & Co.; and the aging Robert Lehman of Lehman Brothers, who retired in the spring of 1968. In fact, those men did help a little: it was Gardner who put Fox in touch with Dillingham. And all three firms apparently worked at finding other possible merger partners for United—at least they drew fees for such efforts: $80,000 apiece in 1967. But, oddly, none knew about the AMK move in advance, or was able to devise much in the way of counterstrategy.

Like Fox himself, most United Fruit shareholders knew nothing of what was coming until that day in September when the AMK block was traded. As it turned out, another company had begun laying its plans for a tender offer for United Fruit before that time. The day after the AMK trade, a group of executives from Zapata Norness Inc. came to Boston to tell Fox that they too wanted to make a tender for his company. This was the offer that forced Black to act before he could make his usual well-mannered overture.

The leading Zapata executive involved was Robert H. Gow, the thirty-six-year-old executive vice president. He saw United Fruit's farming business as a logical extension of his own company's activities in offshore drilling, dredging, shipping, construction, and fish meal. But his determined, sharply analytical mind was more attracted by the financing aspects than the operational similarities between the two companies.

Zapata's first proposal was a $50 ten-year note, plus three-sevenths of a share of Zapata's common stock, for every share of United Fruit. When the idea of debt-laden Zapata's giving its I.O.U. met with resistance in financial circles, Gow changed his tactic. He made another offer through Lehman Brothers—the same Lehman Brothers that was represented on United Fruit's board. The first offer that Zapata filed with the SEC became effective on January 9. Zapata offered a share of a $2 noncumulative preference stock convertible, in a complicated formula, into no more than two Zapata shares. AMK's offer, though not essentially much different, had the advantage that it was more understandable. It would give a $30 convertible debenture, 0.55 share of AMK common and 1.5 AMK warrants. When it became apparent that Zapata's deal wasn't pulling stock, Zapata came up with a better but still complicated offer. But again, all AMK had to do in response was raise the value of its debenture to $38. (Both Zapata and AMK raised their bids on the very day of the big Goldman, Sachs purchase of 360,000 United Fruit shares. Though Goldman, Sachs handled the tender offer for AMK, Gustave Levy says, "I didn't know they were going to raise the bid when we executed that order. I thought they might, and apparently the people who bought the shares guessed that they would too.")

Among the demands made by Zapata that must have annoyed Fox no end was the insistence that it have a majority on United Fruit's board. AMK asked only for minority representation. Finally, on January 27, Zapata withdrew and made a deal with AMK to sell it whatever shares it received for cash up to $3 million, and for notes if more than that came in. AMK also agreed to pay Zapata's cost of soliciting the shares. Both Black and Gow admit that they had previously discussed the sale of AMK's block to Zapata for a price that, under certain circumstances, might have reached $130 a share.

The Public Side

In a letter to shareholders in early October, signed by Fox and Cornuelle, shortly after the second Zapata tender offer, United Fruit said, "Your company is not for sale; it is not on the auction block." The letter said nothing about the offer from AMK, since Black had insisted he would make no offer public without the support of United Fruit's management.

On October 18, in a letter that also contained third-quarter earnings figures (they were down from the year before), shareholders were told about the prospect of another Dillingham bid, but it was noted that none had yet been registered. By that time, Dillingham had released two proposals. The first, estimated then at around $85 worth of securities, would have given United Fruit shareholders three-quarters of a share of a $2 cumulative convertible preferred stock and 0.8 share of common. The second, worth something over $90 at that time, called for a trade of two shares of common and 0.3 of a $3 cumulative convertible preferred. United Fruit's management announced that "Dillingham Corp. appears to have objectives and opportunities in common with United Fruit." Finally, they also made public mention of the AMK block, but said that shareholders would get no AMK offer unless the company's management approved it. The concluding comment was "Keep your cool." Dillingham pulled out a few days later.

In early November, United Fruit's managers were "very pleased" to advise stockholders that the company had found a friend—Textron, Inc.—to save it from AMK. They didn't put it quite that way when they described the proposed consolidation of United Fruit with Textron, but their relief was apparent enough. Textron would, in effect, offer two shares of its common for every share of United Fruit. That was a fine deal for United Fruit shareholders, since Textron and United shares had been selling at just about the same price. Textron's president, G. William Miller, rationalized the deal by demonstrating how Textron was really paying only ten times earnings for United Fruit, when you allowed maybe five years for him to invest its unused assets, compared with more than twenty times once the stock climbed to reflect the competing offers. Miller was so enthusiastic about United Fruit that Textron even hired consultants to help name the new consolidated company—one likely proposal being Centron. But Textron's executives soon discovered that the banana business involved more, as one observed, than "just having dinner with the President of Honduras once in a while." And the company's shareholders complained so bitterly that Miller pulled out in early December.

Gradually, it became apparent that either AMK or Zapata was going to get control of United Fruit. Fox recalls that

"Black had been saying right along that the others would drop out, and he was right. I finally came around to his view that our companies would do well together." So Fox chose Black, dismissing Zapata's offer as "not in the best interest of the shareholders." The contest was over.

In the midst of the battle for control, John Fox reflected that whatever the outcome, his shareholders would do better than he was ever able to do for them. Soon after the original AMK purchase at $56 a share, the stock began climbing. As Zapata and others came into the auction, the price reached as high as $88. And every shareholder who tendered stock to AMK—more than 80 percent of the shares came in—gave up stock that earned a dividend of $1.40 last year in exchange for a debenture that pays $2.09. Besides that, the shareholder received pieces of AMK's future in the form of common stock and warrants, as well as through conversion of the debenture.

A Beneficiary of Evil Days

The company whose independent life ended so suddenly started out as the very model of a dirty young man full of *macho* (the Spanish term for virility). In the years after emancipation the New England ship captains who brought great wealth home to Boston from the slave trade sailed around the world looking for anything else they could haul for profit. They found bananas. Their initial success in selling the fruit on the American seaboard spawned a new wave of conquistadors, who must have ranked among the wildest, greediest men in history. Thousands were willing to brave the swampiest, most disease-ridden jungles of the Americas to clear and drain the land and build railroads and towns to cultivate and ship bananas down to the sea. They died at one another's hands, and from a list of diseases and sins that would hold even the prurient eye of a browser in a Times Square bookstore.

The principal beneficiary of those evil days was United Fruit Co., a combination of four major companies that grew, shipped, and sold the fruit. For years the company was vilified in the countries where it operated as *el pulpo*, the octopus, which had its tentacles in everything, including the selection of governments congenial to its objectives. But today the company is much changed. Still the biggest single employer in the region, it is also the highest agricultural wage payer by far. It has built schools, hospitals, houses, and laboratory facilities.

As United Fruit settles in under AMK's aegis, some antitrust problems may surface. United Fruit has had its own antitrust troubles for a long time. It had to get rid of a railroad in 1962. It still must establish a viable competitor, who will take away about 17 percent of United Fruit's banana business. Moreover, the combination of a big meatpacker (AMK's Morrell subsidiary) and the company still dominant in the banana trade may not sit too well with the antitrust people. What is more, the fact that most of the shares in the original AMK block came from investment funds may make the critics more watchful, even though most of the funds that provided the shares either deny it or insist on anonymity (and Donaldson, Lufkin doesn't tell on its customers). The funds fear criticism that they took too active a role in corporate politics. Yet it is most unlikely that Black would have made the acquisition without their participation. And none of them seems to have gone to United Fruit with offers to sell.

No matter what the Justice Department and the SEC do, the moral of the shotgun wedding is clear enough: Don't trust your institutional shareholders, unless you own more stock than they do, and don't sit on your assets.

Goodrich's Four-Ply Defense

WHEN NORTHWEST INDUSTRIES announced a $1-billion tender offer for B. F. Goodrich last January, many experts considered the case as good as closed. Even though Goodrich is a giant corporation with 1968 sales of $1.1 billion, with forty plants in the United States and interests in twenty-six foreign countries, it looked like easy picking. The Northwest offer, a complicated package of stock, warrants, and debentures, was worth 30 percent more than the market value of Goodrich common stock. But, as Northwest quickly discovered, a take-over is no longer a matter of tempting stockholders and arbitrageurs with a quick profit.

Goodrich was to be helped immeasurably, of course, by a rising anti-merger attitude in Washington. While the Northwest tender offer was in effect, the Justice Department filed an antitrust suit seeking to block the merger. Congress meanwhile announced an impending investigation of conglomerates. And Congressman Wilbur Mills, powerful chairman of the House Ways and Means Committee, introduced legislation to limit the use of interest-bearing debentures in tenders.

Goodrich's efforts to fend off Northwest's take-over rank as a case study in defensive tactics. Shortly after the Northwest offer became public, Jefferson Ward Keener, the dour

157

chairman and chief executive officer of Goodrich, gathered a group of legal, financial, and public-relations experts to stop Northwest. A seven-page confidential memorandum dated January 31, 1969, circulated among five top executives of Goodrich, tells the conclusions the experts reached. "The general consensus of our advisors has remained unchanged," reads the memorandum, "namely that we do not have much chance of warding off Northwest Industries (NW) unless there is some legal quirk that is peculiar to this situation, or unless we merge with a friendly party or parties, which would result in our stockholders getting a better deal than the package NW has offered." The better deal never materialized, but the delaying strategy outlined in the memorandum kept Northwest at bay for months and allowed Washington to come galloping to the rescue of the besieged Akron management.

Among the tactics proposed in the memorandum was the acquisition of a trucking company operating in the area served by the Chicago & North Western Railway, one of Northwest's principal subsidiaries. The idea was to place Goodrich under the jurisdiction of the Interstate Commerce Commission, which in turn might have barred the merger because it would have put Northwest in control of two competing modes of transportation. Several court actions were also recommended, including a suit alleging violations by Northwest of the Securities Exchange Act, and a suit charging infringement of the antitrust act. Goodrich was advised to acquire smaller companies with the idea of getting more than 20 percent of the company's stock in friendly hands, thereby preventing Northwest from filing a consolidated income-tax report. The memorandum noted that the company had already taken steps to alter its arrangements with a group of banks so that a $200-million credit line would be in default in the event that Northwest managed to get control. As the document shows, Goodrich was also considering efforts to have Northwest delisted by the New York Stock Exchange, and hoped to instigate a congressional investigation of "funny-money" take-overs.

Much of the subsequent action followed the Goodrich script. Goodrich acquired a trucking company and asked the ICC to intervene in the take-over fight—a request that was turned down. Northwest had said it would sell the trucking company if it gained control of Goodrich. Stock was placed in friendly hands when Goodrich acquired Gulf Oil's half interest in a jointly owned synthetic rubber plant in exchange for 700,000 of its shares. Stockholders meanwhile approved the classification of directors into three groups, plus a system of cumulative voting designed to keep Northwest from taking immediate control if its tender offer was successful. The stockholders balked, however, at management's proposal that the vote required to permit the acquisition of Goodrich by a company that management opposed be raised from a two-thirds majority of shares outstanding to 80 percent.

"This Is Gross Impropriety!"

In its counterattack, Goodrich was helped by a few serious problems at Northwest. The company began losing money in the first quarter of 1969 because of a strike at its Lone Star Steel Co. and severe weather that affected freight operations on the Chicago & North Western. Northwest stock, which had been selling at $138 a share, had fallen to $105 by the end of February. Moreover, the restrictions in the Mills bill prompted Ben W. Heineman, Northwest's president and chief executive, to revise the terms of his offer by decreasing the amount of debt and by increasing the amount of common stock and warrants in the package.

In May came the news that Goodrich executives had been long awaiting—the Justice Department brought that antitrust suit seeking to enjoin Northwest from acquiring Goodrich. The action was hardly news to Keener and his associates. In February, Goodrich had added to its battery of legal talent the Chicago firm of Chadwell, Keck, Kayser & Ruggles in connection with a suit filed by Northwest that was unrelated to the antitrust case. Richard W. McLaren had resigned from the firm in January to become head of the Justice Department's Antitrust Division. A copy of a letter from McLaren to Northwest's lawyers, dealing with antitrust aspects of the attempted take-over, had been sent to his former colleague, John Chadwell. The letter enabled both Goodrich and Northwest to estimate the date of a possible antitrust suit.

For the Northwest executives, the antitrust suit was the last straw. Heineman felt that his tender offer would have prevailed despite the ingenuity of the Goodrich defense. "This is gross impropriety," said Heineman. "I think Mr. Chadwell should not have accepted the case, or that Mr. McLaren should have disqualified himself." McLaren subsequently replied that the suit was unanimously recommended by members of his staff, and that he had left the Chadwell firm before it was retained by Goodrich. Moreover, he asserted that it is normal to keep all parties advised in such cases.

Over the years Goodrich has been a lackluster performer. Its profits last year were nearly $2 million less than the $46 million earned back in 1955, although sales had increased by 51 percent over the same period. Measured against its competitors in Akron, Goodrich is a poor last. Since 1958, earnings per share have increased at an average annual growth rate of only 2.14 percent, far below the 7.96 percent of Goodyear and the 8.7 percent of Firestone. The Goodrich margin on sales averaged 4.1 percent compared to 4.8 percent for Goodyear and 5.3 percent for Firestone. And the company's 8.1 percent return on invested capital last year lagged far behind Firestone's 12.6 percent and Goodyear's 12.8 percent. The Goodrich management was well aware of its faltering performance, and twice in the past five years made some bold efforts to improve earnings. But none of these efforts was really successful. Even before Northwest Industries made its move, Goodrich was an ideal target for an aggressive conglomerate.

A conservative economist who became chief executive officer in 1958, Chairman Keener for years kept a lid on capital spending at a time when the competition was borrowing heavily to expand. Until recent years, Keener, like his predecessor John Lyon Collyer, disliked the idea of incurring long-term debt, even though cash flow was insufficient to finance expansion at a pace comparable to that of the other rubber companies. On the other hand, Keener had no objection to paying out as much as 76 percent of

Goodrich's earnings to stockholders. One result of niggardly capital spending can be seen in a key statistic. Goodrich labor costs in relation to sales are 35.1 percent, compared to 30.2 percent for Goodyear. For a billion-dollar company, each tenth of a percentage point in cost reductions represents $1 million a year increase in pretax profits.

Though Goodrich is best known as a tire manufacturer, 60 percent of its sales and earnings come from other fields. In the fifties the chemical industry was a logical field of expansion since Goodrich, from the days before World War II when it pioneered in the development of synthetic rubber, had a strong research staff. The most important, and initially the most profitable, venture in chemicals was the manufacture of polyvinyl chloride (PVC), a basic building block in plastics. One of the first companies to market this material, Goodrich priced PVC so that profit margins were extremely high, balm indeed in view of the unexciting profits in the tire business. As new applications were found for the plastic, the market grew rapidly and Goodrich spent heavily to expand production. But more chemical companies, attracted by the high profits and strong growth, began making PVC and prices tumbled sharply. In 1954 general-purpose PVC sold for 38 cents a pound; last year the average price was 10 cents. Goodrich is still the world's largest producer of PVC and has the lowest-cost manufacturing process, but there is a widespread belief that its pricing policies of the fifties (set by Keener's predecessor) may have invited competitors into the field too soon.

A more recent effort in chemicals has been unsuccessful, at least so far. In the mid-sixties scientists at the Goodrich research center near Akron developed a poromeric material with many of the characteristics of Du Pont's Corfam. After some development work, a pilot plant was begun, and the product, named Aztran, seemed commercially salable. In 1967 a multi-million-dollar plant was built in Marietta, Ohio, and salesmen began making the rounds of shoe manufacturers. Sales were disappointing, however, since Goodrich offered Aztran for men's shoes only, while Du Pont had developed several kinds of Corfam that conformed in price and appearance to the many kinds of leather available.

Although an effort is now being made to develop a range similar to Corfam, Goodrich executives are considering the possibility of writing off the Aztran adventure.

Goodrich is engaged in a multiplicity of other endeavors. It makes a variety of industrial chemicals, is a major producer of synthetic rubber, and has fourteen industrial-product plants that produce everything from rubber bands to mattresses. About 5 percent of sales come from a footwear division, 5 percent from aerospace, and 2 percent from textiles. Finally, about 13 percent of Goodrich sales come from its international operations.

Rushing the Radial Age

The rapid growth of foreign markets is the most exciting aspect of the tire business these days, but Goodrich is in poor position to cash in on the boom. The company was reluctant to invest heavily abroad after World War II, and even in the fifties its European investment consisted of minority interests in manufacturers, such as Kleber-Colombes in France and Veith in West Germany. Today American companies control a major portion of the foreign tire business, mainly because Firestone and Goodyear saw unparalleled opportunity. These two companies together own or have an interest in sixty-two foreign plants, while Goodrich controls seven and has minority interests in five others. Goodrich's first wholly owned European tire plant, located in West Germany, began full production only a few months ago.

In its tire business at home Goodrich has blown hot and cold. When Goodyear cut tire prices by 10 to 15 percent in 1959, Goodrich was handicapped with high-cost, inefficient plants, the legacy of the company's pinchpenny policies. Not until 1962 did it build a modern plant in Fort Wayne, Indiana, and by then the competition had taken away a good slice of the business. (The decline in Goodrich's market share is well known in the industry, though rubber companies refuse to give any figures.) Moreover, Goodrich depended heavily on sales of original-equipment tires to Detroit auto manufacturers and allowed the competition to cream the larger and more lucrative replacement market. Firestone and Goodyear both spent heavily to build their own outlets, while

Goodrich made a stab at improving its marketing strength by making two small acquisitions in 1961—Rayco Stores with 124 outlets, and Vanderbilt Tire, which had franchise arrangements with department stores in major cities. Vanderbilt was sold in 1965, and with Rayco Goodrich has about half as many retail outlets as either Firestone or Goodyear. Yet it must mount a costly national advertising program to keep up with these two giants.

At times Goodrich has run its tire business as if it wanted sales at any price. Consider the Goodrich tactics in bidding to supply tires for Detroit's municipally owned buses. In such cases tire companies try to sell contractual mileage accounts, under which fleet owners lease tires with charges based on tire usage. For thirty-five years Uniroyal had won the contract, but in 1963, Goodrich won with a bid worth $1,450,000 over five years, about $195,000 below Uniroyal. That low bid was enhanced by the elimination of a wage escalation clause, which the other companies considered necessary because of the certainty of higher labor costs. Last year Goodrich won the contract again by bidding at the same price, and it must absorb all wage increases granted until 1973. Goodrich insists that it is breaking even on the contract. But a competitor who dropped out of the bidding insists that it is impossible to make a profit at Goodrich's price.

Two years ago Goodrich made an expensive gamble in an effort to improve its position in the tire industry. Believing that Detroit would adopt a European-style radial tire as standard equipment on many new cars in 1971, Goodrich tooled up for what appeared to be a large and profitable market. The radial tire requires special manufacturing equipment and techniques, and Goodrich plunged ahead. The other tire makers, however, chose to put their bets on the belted bias tire, a reinforced version of the conventional two-ply tire.

While acknowledging the radial tire's safer riding characteristics and longer mileage, Detroit's experts had two objections to the Goodrich tire. First, it costs considerably more than conventional equipment. More important, engineers felt that radials (highly popular in Europe) were incompatible with the suspension systems of the best-selling American cars, producing a harsh ride. But even if the riding characteristics of the tire were acceptable, it is doubtful that the automobile companies would feel comfortable with a single source of supply. The fact that Goodyear, Firestone, and others failed to build sizable capacity for making the radial tire probably doomed in advance the Goodrich idea of selling radials as original equipment. While still insisting on the superiority of the radial tire, Goodrich now concedes that the belted bias tire will be standard equipment on most American-made cars in the years just ahead.

Springing the Trap

When Heineman took a look at Goodrich last fall, he saw a matchless opportunity for a major acquisition. A staff group headed by Howard A. Newman, chairman of the board of Northwest, had made a lengthy analysis of Goodrich. It had a low debt-equity ratio, and despite its wobbly earnings record, an important position in both the chemical and the tire industries. Heineman believed that the company, with its untapped earnings potential, was undervalued by the investment community. Most important of all, Heineman concluded that the company's poor performance was attributable to the lack of an aggressive management.

Heineman hesitated for about two months to move on Goodrich, partly because he also had his eye on another company. Without revealing the name, he had received the approval of Northwest's board for open-market purchases in Interchemical (which has since changed its name to Inmont), a New York-based chemical company with sales of $317 million and earnings of $14,200,000. After accumulating just under 10 percent of Interchemical stock, Heineman called on President James T. Hill to inform him of that fact, and to tell him that Northwest had not decided what course of action to pursue. It was clear from the conversation, however, that Hill would have rebuffed any take-over bid.

On December 23 the executive committee of the Northwest board approved the purchase of 350,000 shares, or about 2.5 percent of the shares then outstanding. One of the board members, Laurence A. Tisch, chairman and chief executive officer of Loew's Theatres Inc., was playing tennis that day at his Paradise Island hotel in the Bahamas. His game was interrupted by a telephone call from Newman, who asked his approval of the purchase and described the reasons for the investment. "There's no need to go through all that, Mickey," said Tisch. "I know all about that company. We have a large position." As it happened, Loew's had been buying Goodrich stock for a number of months and had accumulated 358,450 shares. From that point on, however, Loew's stopped buying. Goodrich has since charged that Heineman and Tisch were acting in collusion in their stock purchases. Both are vehement in their denials. "It simply looked to me as if Goodrich had little downside risk," says Tisch. "It just looked like a good investment."

The heavy buying in Goodrich stock attracted the attention of John L. Weinberg, a Goodrich director and a partner in Goldman, Sachs. The previous June, Weinberg had arranged a meeting between Keener and Delbert W. Coleman, who then was president of Seeburg Corp., a jukebox manufacturer. Coleman wanted to present a merger idea to Goodrich. The proposal was rejected, but Weinberg recalls that he warned Keener, "Ward, this is the kind of world you're living in today." On January 9, Tisch disclosed that Loew's had a position in Goodrich, and although he disclaimed any intention of making a tender offer, the atmosphere in Akron grew tense. "I didn't try to hide my investment in Goodrich," says Tisch. "I was buying in the fall through Goldman, Sachs." However, neither Keener nor Weinberg could be sure that Loew's alone was responsible for all the buying of Goodrich stock.

At that point, Keener decided that Goodrich should think of opening negotiations with potential merger partners of its own choice. That triggered an episode of comic misadventure that is a source of embarrassment to some of the participants, and there are conflicting versions of the incident. Apparently misunderstanding the instructions of a Goodrich executive, the accounting firm of Ernst & Ernst, which had previously been commissioned to seek acquisitions for Goodrich, asked Lehman Brothers to suggest companies that might be suitably combined with its Akron client.

At a dinner party in New York on Friday, January 10, three weeks after Northwest had begun buying Goodrich stock, Robert McCabe, a partner in Lehman Brothers, was a dinner guest of Alan Patricof, assistant to the chairman of the board of Northwest Industries. Patricof was dumfounded when the man from Lehman Brothers asked if Northwest might be interested in making a deal with Goodrich. At that point Northwest owned 156,000 shares of Goodrich. With understandable eagerness, Patricof led his guest to a telephone and McCabe had a lengthy conversation with Stephen Dubrul, another Lehman Brothers partner. As a result, Lehman Brothers recommended that Ernst & Ernst propose Northwest to the Goodrich management.

The real intentions of Goodrich at that point are known only to Keener and his associates. Heineman, however, took the Lehman Brothers proposal at face value, a signal that the Akron management was ready to talk. He therefore requested that Northwest be given the first opportunity to negotiate with Goodrich. But Lehman Brothers could not give preferential treatment to Northwest, saying only that the company's name would be submitted along with about a dozen others. And however much Heineman may have wanted a confidential chat with Keener, the ethical conventions of the financial world prevented Northwest from bypassing the two middlemen and making its offer directly to Goodrich.

Unknown to Heineman, his interest was conveyed almost immediately to Goodrich anyway. During a flight from New York to Akron on Monday, January 13, John Hart, Goodrich's vice controller and a vice president, was informed of the Northwest proposal by an executive from Ernst & Ernst. Hart dismissed the idea, saying vaguely that Goodrich had no intention of going into the railroad business. For some unaccountable reason, Hart failed to report the Northwest proposal to Keener. That breakdown in communication was to become an angry point of dispute in the events that followed.

The Mice Were Nibbling on Wall Street

Fearful that some other company might close a deal with Goodrich, the Northwest executives began to think in terms of a tender offer. They decided that an exchange of common stock, warrants, and debentures worth between $75 and $80 for each share of Goodrich common would be attractive enough to gain control. Goodrich stock had been selling in the forties for the last half of 1968, but under the pressure of buying by Northwest had risen to the mid-fifties. However, Heineman had not yet decided whether, or when, he would make an announcement of a tender offer. He still hoped that a friendly deal might be arranged.

Heineman's hand was forced on Friday, January 17. Gustave Levy of Goldman, Sachs telephoned Heineman and said, "Ben, it's all over the Street that you're going to make a tender offer for Goodrich. Is it true?" After a pause, Heineman replied, "I can't comment on that." A few minutes later, an agitated Levy called again with the same question and received this enigmatic reply: "I wouldn't want to put a friend of mine in a position of conflict of interest." Heineman realized that unless he made an announcement of a tender offer, he might be in violation of both SEC and New York Stock Exchange rules on disclosure, and he released the news before the opening of the New York Stock Exchange on Monday, January 20. "I knew on Friday that we had to move," Heineman recalled later. "The mice were nibbling all over Wall Street and both Northwest and Goodrich stocks were rising."

Keener was infuriated when he read the details of the Northwest offer that morning. "They have started off on the wrong foot," he said, "regardless of whether or not their proposal has any merit." Heineman says he tried to soften the blow by telephoning Keener that morning prior to publication of the offer, but was unable to reach him. Moreover, Heineman waved the olive branch in his press release by stating that Northwest had no intention of altering the Goodrich management. In a further gesture of conciliation, Larry Tisch told Gus Levy that Northwest would propose a new exchange offer if Goodrich was willing to make a friendly deal, and that there was a chance that Goodrich could be the surviving company. Keener rebuffed these overtures. A Goodrich director says, "Heineman knew where the hell we were. If he really wanted to be friendly—well, you don't sneak around behind someone and hit him over the head with a baseball bat, and then run around in front and say that you want to be his friend."

Heineman replies that the Goodrich management is confused about the sequence of events and seems to regard the use of a tender offer as a kind of antisocial act. "In expressing our interest through Lehman Brothers," says Heineman, "a respected investment-banking firm that had been engaged to find a merger partner for Goodrich, we believed that we were going to them directly. But, in any event, Goodrich has unparalleled arrogance in assuming that we first had to make an offer to management. We've gone to the *owners* of a business and said, 'We would like to make you an offer which you are free to accept or reject as you choose.' We haven't used coercion. We haven't bludgeoned anybody directly."

A Glacial Summit in Akron

Despite the public rebuff by Keener, Heineman wanted to make one more effort to make a friendly deal with Goodrich. "It's not my style to raid anyone," he says. "We were still prepared to sit down and work out an arrangement." Three days after the announcement of his tender offer, Heineman, accompanied by Gaylord Freeman Jr., chairman and chief executive of the First National Bank of Chicago and a director of Northwest, journeyed to Akron to meet with Keener. The atmosphere was glacial. Keener sat behind his bare desk, along with Raphael Jeter, the chief counsel for Goodrich. To Keener's assertion that Heineman had not contacted him prior to the announcement, Heineman asked, "Didn't Lehman Brothers tell you?" After forty-five minutes it was clear to Heineman that Keener was determined to fight. "Mr. Keener had made up his mind that he didn't want any part of Northwest," says Heineman. "I thought him a very restricted man—that he'd been weaned too early as a baby." Keener says he cannot remember what he thought of Heineman.

In a letter sent to stockholders in February, Keener said it had been hinted that he could become the chairman of the combined companies. "I rejected this approach out of hand," he wrote. "I could not place my own position ahead of your interests and those of over 47,000 employees, and neither would any other member of your management." Officers and directors of Northwest insist that no such offer was made.

Later Keener wrote to stockholders, "We want you to know that no member of the board and no corporate officer plans to exchange his shares and none of us has sold B. F. Goodrich shares since the offer was announced last January." The directors of Goodrich, however, owned only 55,465 shares among them, or .04 percent of the outstanding shares. Moreover, in the five-year period up to February 1, Keener, President Harry Warner, and Group Vice President William Perdriau had acquired little stock in their own company; they exercised the right to buy only 2,052 of the 45,700 shares granted under a stock-option plan.

For Heineman, the Goodrich take-over was intended to be the climax of three extraordinary careers. First, he was a successful lawyer. Then, in 1956, he was elected chairman of the Chicago & North Western Railway, a dying operation that became a big money spinner under Heineman's imaginative direction. (The North Western is probably the only road that makes money on its commuter hauls.) Heineman then set out to put together the largest railroad combination (in terms of mileage) in the nation. He acquired about 90 percent of the stock in the Milwaukee Road, and made an attempt to gain control of the Rock Island. The idea was to merge the three railroads into one midwestern system that would connect the powerful Penn Central in the East and Union Pacific in the West. Other railroads oppose the plan, which is pending before the ICC.

Heineman switched direction again in 1967, when he transformed his railroad into a holding company called Northwest Industries. The following year he negotiated a merger with Philadelphia & Reading Corp. (P. & R.), a successful conglomerate that had increased per-share earnings by an annual average rate of 11.22 percent in the decade up through 1967. P. & R. was a combination of medium-sized companies making consumer and industrial products that had been put together by Howard A. Newman from the dying embers of an old anthracite business. So high was Newman's reputation in banking circles that he had raised an $80-million credit line without collateral to buy Lone Star Steel. Now the biggest component of Northwest Industries, P. & R. accounted for 50 percent of its 1968 sales and 89 percent of its pretax profits excluding nonrecurring items.

With this merger, Heineman suddenly became an aggressive conglomerater. He made an attempt to acquire Home Insurance, but lost when City Investing topped his bid. However, he had the consolation of making a $16-million profit after taxes from the initial open-market purchases of Home Insurance stock. An attempt to merge with Swift came to nothing when Heineman decided that the value he had seen in the company was illusory. The stage was then set for another attempt at a major acquisition.

Heineman had his own reasons for moving fast. He had about made up his mind to wind up his business career within two years, possibly to enter government service, or to write a book on the nation's transportation problems. Says Heineman, "You come to a point in your life when you ask yourself, 'What do you want to do? Do you just want to keep on making bigger companies out of littler ones?'" But before he left business, he wanted to turn Northwest into a major industrial entity, and the Northwest-Goodrich combination fitted his personal timetable nicely.

Like a Cyanide Pill

Shortly after the Northwest announcement, Keener assembled three law firms, two public-relations counselors, two investment-banking companies, and an accountant to advise him on the fine art of fending off Northwest. A lawyer's most effective defense against a take-over is to prevent the registration of securities offered in exchange for the stock of the target company. White & Case, Goodrich's regular attorneys, sought to accomplish this by asking various state securities commissions to prohibit the registration of debentures and warrants offered by Northwest on the grounds that the offer was in violation of states' security laws.

But the White & Case analysis of Northwest's registration statement contained an extraordinary blunder. The law firm claimed that the company's existing debt-equity ratio was 75 to 1 and that the ratio would increase to more than 160 to 1 if the maximum $689 million in Northwest debentures was issued for the Goodrich stock. Apparently, White & Case arrived at these figures by dividing an inflated amount of Northwest debt by the number of shares outstanding instead of comparing the dollar amounts of debt and equity. Northwest's debt-equity ratio at the time was 40 percent to 60 percent equity, and even using the erroneous debt figure cited by White & Case, the ratio, assuming complete acceptance of the exchange offer, would be 55 percent debt to 45 percent equity. Raphael Jeter, the Goodrich general counsel, claims that the letter was mailed without his knowledge. "I never saw it," he says. "We were so busy here in Akron that I didn't know whether we were walking or running." The White & Case attempt to bar registration of Northwest's securities failed in every state.

The difficulties that B. F. Goodrich faced in trying to make a defensive merger are spelled out in that January 31 memorandum that summed up the brainstorming sessions of the experts. The memorandum suggested that "the desirable growth rate of a company to be acquired should be based on the performance of Firestone, Goodyear, and Uniroyal and not B.F.G." A starkly candid analysis stated the problems that would arise if Goodrich acquired a number of small companies. "This will require," said the memo, "that we (1) view the footwear and industrial products industries as nongrowth industries, (2) withhold substantial capital expenditures for the tire company until it demonstrates that it can produce a satisfactory earnings growth, and (3) channel our cash flow into the new firms acquired." Seldom has a major corporation been so frank about its own weaknesses.

Of all the tactics devised by management to fend off Northwest, none was so extreme as the revision of Goodrich's bank-credit agreement. On February 3, thirteen days after Heineman announced his tender offer, Goodrich increased its line of credit with twenty-one banks, headed by First National City, to $250 million, and at the same time amended the agreement so that the loan would be in default in the event of a take-over. Moreover, the company, according to the memorandum, was considering using up to $200 million of the loan to prepay such items as income taxes and accounts payable, and to make contributions to retirement funds. The intent was "to drive home to Mr. Heineman the fact that he will have to make arrangements to borrow this amount of money elsewhere in advance of the close of his tender offer."

The details of this extreme maneuver were revealed by the Goodrich lawyers during the final minutes of the Justice Department's antitrust case in Chicago last month. Judge Hubert L. Will was astonished. Likening the amendment to a "Herman Goering cyanide pill," Judge Will wondered why Goodrich would voluntarily enter into an agreement "under which it threatened to commit financial suicide in the event that this transaction is consummated. It's a shocking document. It's the worst indictment of Goodrich's management of anything in the record in this case."

The Northwest-Goodrich battle is a landmark in more ways than one. It was the Justice Department's first attempt to enjoin a would-be raider, and the first court hearing in its attempt to extend antitrust laws to include mergers and acquisitions that could result in concentration of manufacturing assets. After listening to the opening arguments, Judge Will said, "We are really faced with a whole new dimension of value judgments here."

To Ben Heineman, caught in the storm, the events of the past five months suggest a climate of management fear in many corporations. "At the moment," he says, "we are in the grip of an hysteria rising largely out of fear on the part of insecure and inadequate managements that's contrary to the best interests of stockholders. This fear may prevent shareowners from exercising appropriate control over the officers and directors who represent them. It may prevent them from realizing the true value of their securities. And I believe that there's going to be a time when many people will regret the extreme positions they are now taking, especially in stimulating the government to action."

But Ward Keener showed no signs of regret at all.

Index